Lynda Benglis

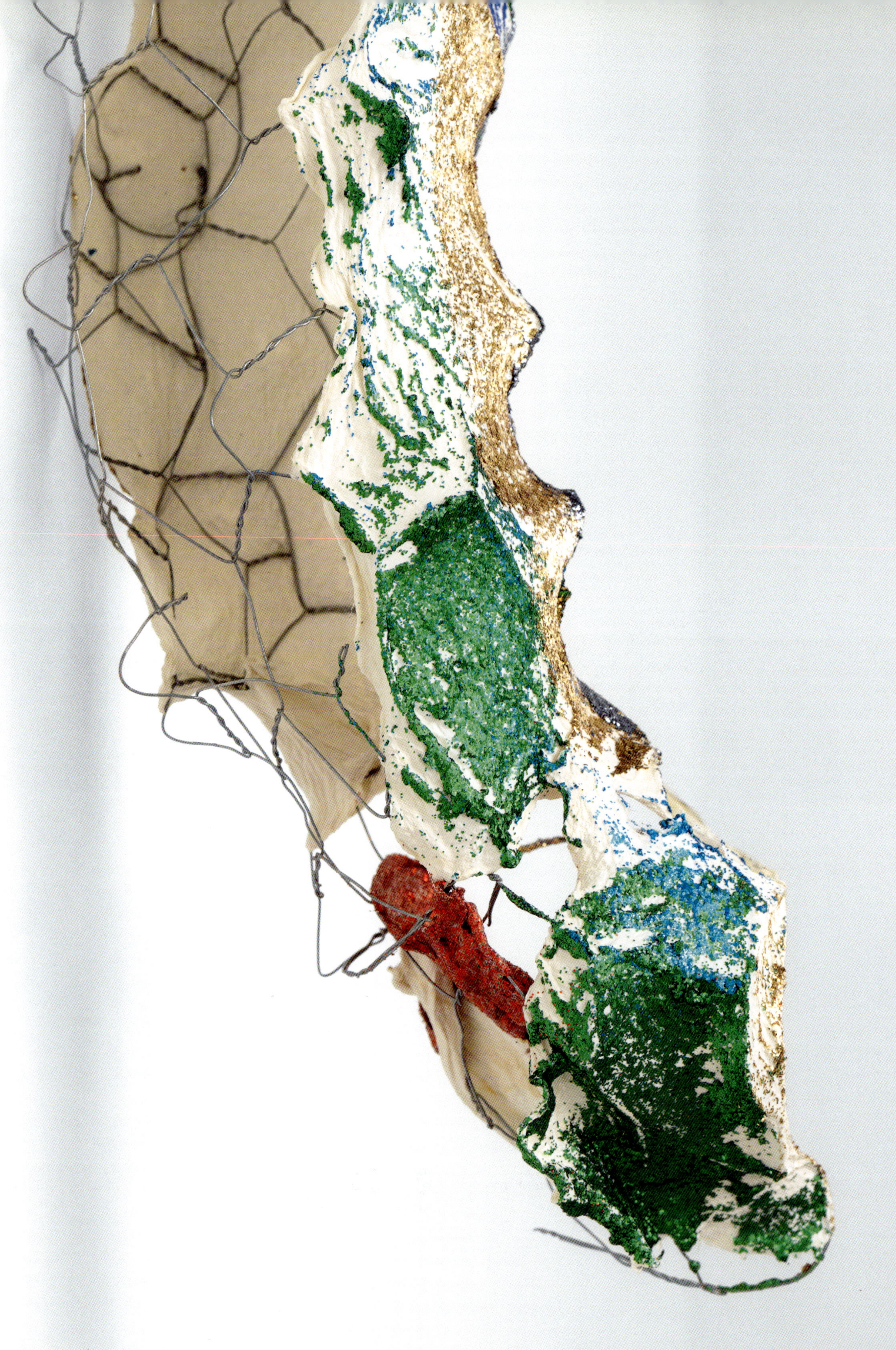

Lynda Benglis

Cheim & Read

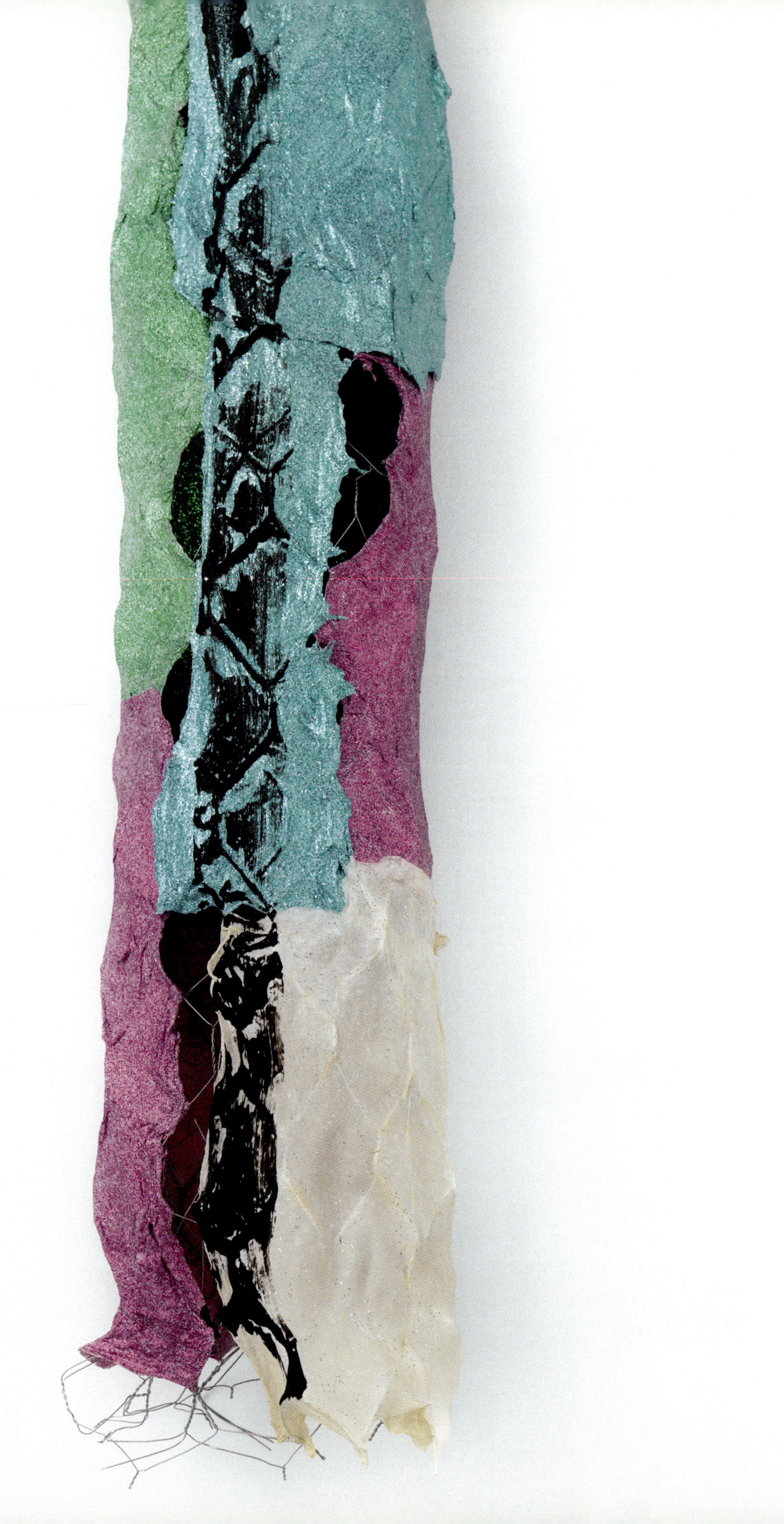

EVERY FORCE EVOLVES A FORM

Nancy Princenthal

A sense of bounty and ease has long contended, in Lynda Benglis's work, with vivifying evidence of strenuous physicality. "I like to work in a way that the image flows" from qualities inherent to the material, she explained some three decades ago,[1] suggesting a process of fluid spontaneity. In the same interview, she said that being immersed in the medium at hand could be a little overwhelming, "like wrestling with your sheets as you come out of a dream."[2] Together these reflections capture the physical and expressive freedom, and the exertion, that have characterized Benglis's work since the latex paint pours of the late nineteen-sixties and the polyurethane foam mounds that followed shortly thereafter: on the one hand, psychedelic colors and boundary-trouncing forms, and on the other the muscular business—witness, for example, the deployment of five-gallon paint cans for the pours—of bringing that ebullience into being.

Benglis's new work, created with handmade paper, continues to reflect both serendipity and fierce determination. It involves applying soaked paper to chicken wire armatures, and requires both grace and strength. Pulling and twisting the armatures into shape is a demanding job that requires a partner; "it's like dancing,"[3] she says, using a favorite analogy. Indeed, one new sculpture, called *The Dancer*, comes close to explicit representation of the subject, with its graceful allusions to erect torso, bent arm and twisting thigh. More typical are abstract compositions animated by the vigorous torque that, Benglis also notes, is characteristic of the paper sculptures, a dynamic that supports their suggestion of restless movement. "There's no up or down with the work," she says, nor a front or back. "They're composed from every angle," and the space visible between their components is as important as the positive forms.

Benglis has used paper before: in 1980 she created a series of bowtie-shaped cast paper sculptures, and in 2001 undertook another experiment in cast paper, working with a foam mold. Using paper as skin, as she is doing now, is new; she remarks on the connection to animal hides. But in some of the recent work, in which the paper pulp is saturated with glitter in evening-gown shades of aqua, pink, purple and green as well as copper, bronze, silver and gold, the result is gleaming surfaces that are, as she says, like mercury. Stretched taut over the metal webbing, the glitter-imbued paper produces effects that are somewhere between scaly and sequined, gaudy and glamorous. The title of the brightly multicolored *Gone Harlequin* points to the diamond patterning that is impressed on these works' surface by their wire scaffolds, and in turn to the Rabelaisian Carnival from which harlequin costumes descend. Yet most of Benglis's current

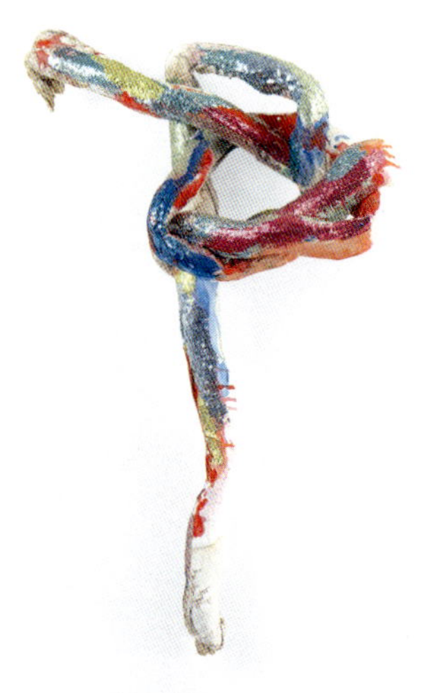

Sparkle Knot V, 1972, aluminum screen, cotton bunting, plaster, acrylic paint and sparkles, 42 x 25 x 13 in

materials are decidedly down to earth—paper, after all, is made from vegetable matter and water—and includes coal dust bound in water. Brushed onto the surfaces of some sculptures in brusque, calligraphic marks of the deepest black, the coal-based paint carries a hint of lightless depths—and also, as in the rugged *Charred Sparkle Glory*, a measure of not-quite-extinguished fire. Often, both coal-black calligraphy and glitter—along with acrylic paint in a wide variety of colors—complement each other in a single work.

Although the glitter-imbued paper is also new, Benglis has used sparkles before, too. Sometimes it suggests the glint of light on water; in purely formal terms, it can refract and atomize color, further destabilizing already active surfaces. But many of its references are cultural. The series of painted canvas *Sparkle Knots* of the early nineteen-seventies, dusted with glitter, can seem at once girlishly innocent and raucously honky-tonk; both impressions were heightened when some of the *Knots* were installed in the Clocktower gallery, in New York, in 1973, surrounded by twinkly little Christmas lights. And as with the gilding Benglis applied to the svelte, mermaid-finned sculptures of the late seventies—Rene Ricard referred to them as "what Venus would wear to the disco on Olympus"[4]—her use of glitter has kindred in such decorative work of the seventies as Miriam Schapiro's lavishly patterned "femmages," Joyce Kozloff's dazzling mosaics, and the ribbons and bunting in painted and sculpted imagery by Ree Morton. Benglis, who was born and raised in Louisiana and has residences on three continents, was in Los Angeles early in that formative decade, and was involved there in the feminist community led by Schapiro, Judy Chicago and their Cal Arts students. While never explicitly political, nor, for that matter, fixedly gendered, Benglis's work remains animated by an energy that is undeniably sensual.

And now as in the seventies, her sexual politics are leavened by a renegade sense of humor. Referring to the women's movement, Benglis once said, "I appreciated the revered attitude and the seriousness, but I also wanted more playfulness."[5]

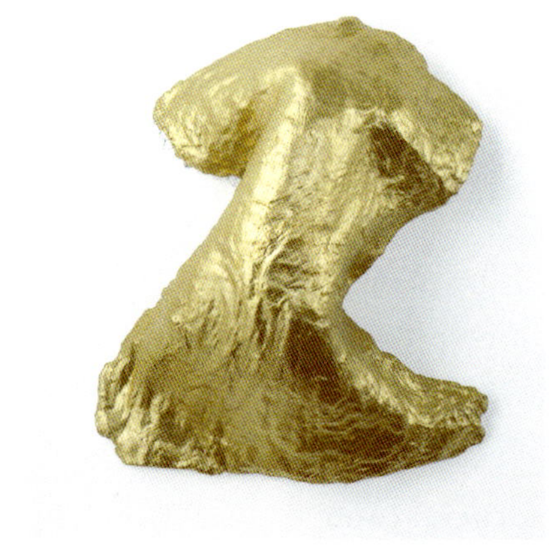

Figure 4, 1978, chicken wire, cotton, plaster, gesso and gold leaf, 30 1/2 x 25 x 10 1/2 in

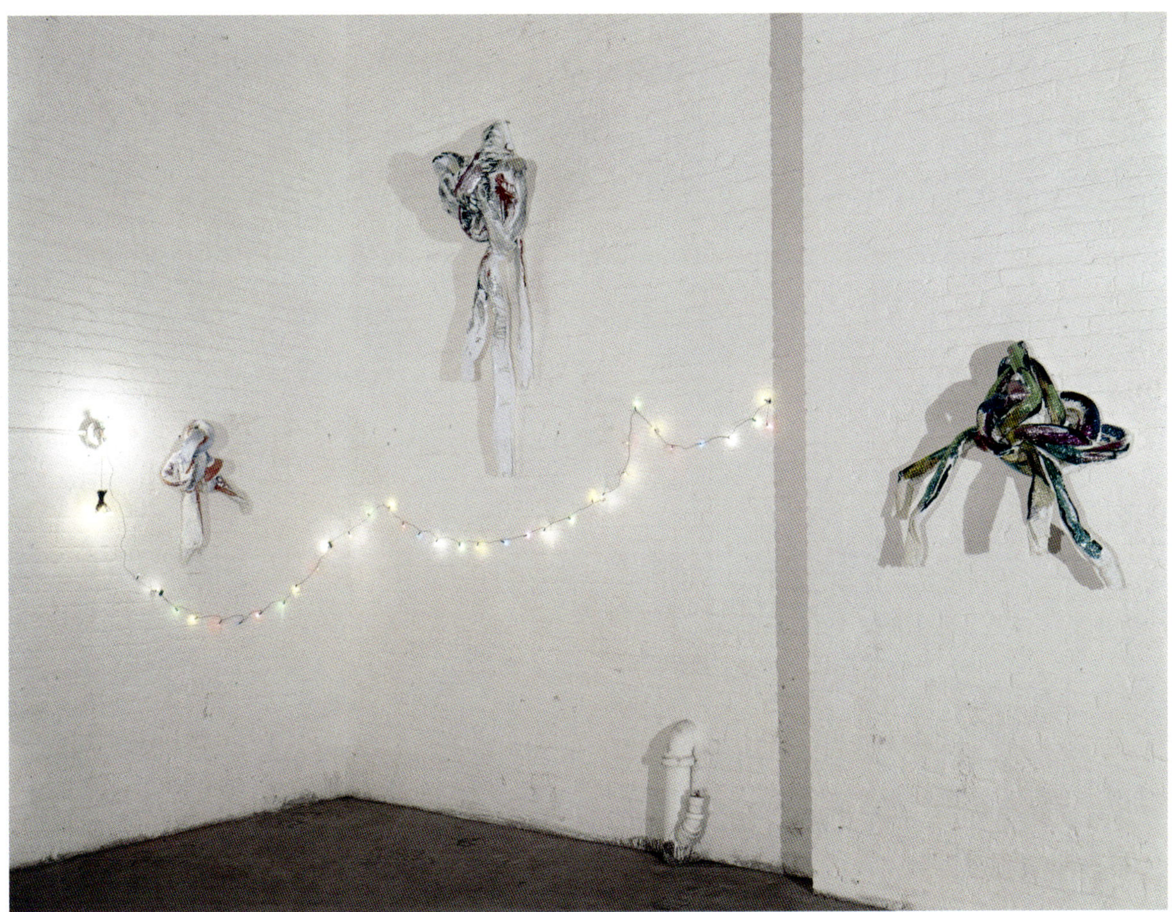

The Clocktower, New York, December 6, 1973–January 20, 1974

(Similarly, in response to a question about the origin of the new work's titles, she says she often favors those that are funny.) It is perhaps the mounded foam sculptures that come closest to physical comedy, their alarmingly expanding forms recalling the famous *I Love Lucy* episode that finds Lucy putting too much yeast in her dough; the bread pushes out the oven door and then overtakes the kitchen. A hint of rage powers the irresistible silliness of the classic episode, with its premonitory note of housewives in rebellion. Of course, the lasting appeal of Lucy's antics is partly fueled by camp, a quality, definitively analyzed by Susan Sontag, that has been noted in Benglis's work as well.[6] She shares it with other artists whose work favors bangles and beads, from John Torreano's jeweled paintings to Thomas Lanigan-Schmidt's lavishly decorated altarpieces. Like them, Benglis has never been afraid of being dismissed as vulgar— witness the giant double-headed dildo with which she posed, naked, for a photograph published in *Artforum* in 1974 that at times has threatened to eclipse her art. That image's crucial (and still contested) place in cultural history obscures its rollicking humor—and, even more, its call to sheer physical enjoyment, whether sexual or visual. "The decorative sense and the pleasure we receive from it is very basic to the human situation,"[7] Benglis says, noting that we share it with birds and other animals. Of all the sensations her work evokes, pure delight is among the keenest.

That is not to deny its engagement with Modernist history. If some of the current paper sculptures can be compared to freestanding brushstrokes, suspended in midair, they have been launched there by her work's earliest impulse, to give volume and movement to paint. And that impulse, as she has said, is in part a response to Pollock's performative methods, and those of his Color Field heirs (*Hey Hey Frankenthaler*, one of Benglis's poured paintings is subtitled). "Pollock pioneered the movement of dealing with materials used by the artist as the prime manifestation of imagery," said Benglis early on. "He drew with paint by dipping sticks into cans of liquid color and making an image on canvas placed on the floor." Clearly, this "way of thinking,"[8] as Benglis called it, was a lesson to her; so, it seems, was his use of metallic paint and lavishly filigreed surfaces. Art historian T. J. Clark writes that in the crucial years of 1947–50, when Pollock initiated the dripped and splattered compositions, his titles—*Magic Lantern*, *Sea Change*, *Phosphorescence*, *Shimmering Substance*, *Watery Paths*, *Lucifer*—drew from a language of "magic and release: richness, incrustation, sea change, an endless plunging (like Lucifer) through the heavens." Clark says Pollock's world of that time was characterized by "delight, [by] fullness and strangeness—suspension of gravity, the slow turn of things in a green sea, the impossible gray fire of phosphorescence off Accabonac Harbor."[9] One thinks of Benglis's *Misty Drawing* (plate 20), its surfaces dappled with glittery, Pollockian patches of gleaming gray and lavender, its contours mobile to the point of indeterminacy. But Clark's lush language suits all of Benglis's new work, which so often seems to tumble and float, remarkably well.

Last among the constituent elements of the new paper sculptures is the chicken wire that gives them shape—and, when pried apart and exposed, as in the spiky, bronze and pink *Feminine Fork* (plate 26), some rather sharp edges. A humble material, it seems meant to be concealed, like undergarments—

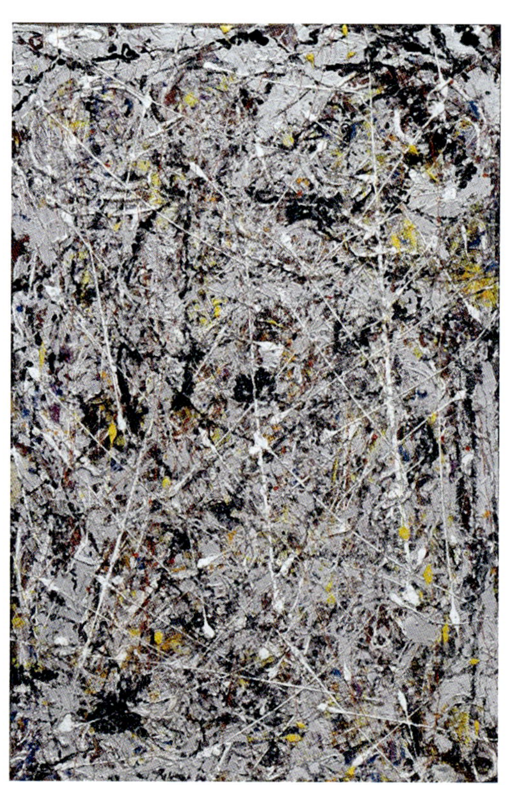

Jackson Pollock, *Phosphorescence*, 1947, oil, enamel and aluminum paint on canvas, 44 x 28 in
Collection Addison Gallery of American Art

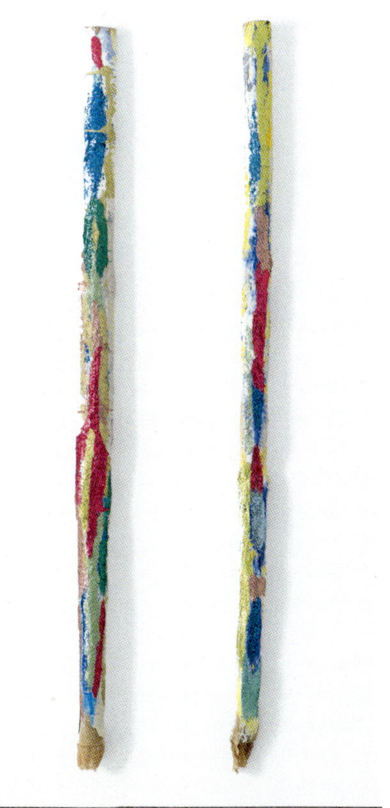

Hoofers I, 1971–72, aluminum screen, red cotton bunting, plaster, gesso, acrylic and glitter, 102 x 5 1/2 x 4 in

Hoofers II, 1971–72, aluminum screen, red cotton bunting, plaster, gesso, acrylic and glitter, 102 x 4 1/2 x 3 in

corsets, stays—or such infrastructural elements as metal rebar. The flared top of *Fan Dance* reveals, with a gesture like a quickly opened fan, or the petticoat-revealing kick of a high-stepping dancer, a glimpse of wire screen. Benglis's use of such wire mesh goes back to *Hoofers I* and *Hoofers II* (1971–72), their roughly cylindrical, limblike forms made of mesh covered with bunting and plaster that was then painted.[10] The glittery *Hoofers* (the word is vaudeville slang for dancers), as Susan Krane has remarked, "barely graze the floor,"[11] sustaining an active weightlessness that has a clear kinship to the paper sculptures. Similar, too, is the often tubular new work's reflection of the proportion and shape of the artist's limbs— and of gesture, and dance. Though the challenge to gravity made by the paper sculptures is less dramatic than, say, her cantilevered installations of 1971, which in some cases glowed in the dark, many of the new works are powerfully buoyant. Benglis acknowledges their evocations of birds— one recent wing-shaped sculpture is titled *Swift* (plate 17); others suggest peacocks' iridescent plumage, and still others nests, hives and cocoons, as in *Bronze Cacoon*, which fairly squirms with incipient life.

Benglis also affirms a kinship, in some, with kites, an affection for which was born in childhood (her father made them by hand) and enhanced by attending the annual kite festivals of Ahmedabad, where she has had a home since 1979. There are hints in the new works of shattered piñatas, as in *Broken Favor I* and *II* (plates 9 and 7), which in turn evoke the kind of unexpected gift—of little treats that come before and after an already abundant celebration—that in Louisiana is known as *lagniappe* (a term Benglis has used as a title for a series of sculptures). In keeping with earlier work, those of the new sculptures that are roughly cylindrical also have more erotic associations, evoking phalluses and vaginas (considered as tubes, one becomes the other). They have something of the genially robust, hermaphroditic quality of Louise Bourgeois's well-known *Fillette* (1968), an oversize phallus that doubles as a long-necked female bust.[12] But as often as Benglis embraces the Dionysian, she promotes the Apollonian in her work, as when she describes herself as a Classicist, and points out her connection to both ancient and modern Greece, where her paternal grandparents were born. Among the influences she cites for the *Sparkle Knots* are such altogether chaste sources as braided Easter bread, Greek May Day wreaths, and the gold and gilded accessories of the Greek Orthodox Church as well as Classical caryatids. Windblown chitons, fluty and high-waisted, as well as classical columns with scrolled capitals and bases, can be seen in many new works, such as *Curtains* (plate 15) and *Flying Fern*.

Many of these associations confirm the importance of place in the ongoing development of Benglis's vocabulary. Her early exposure to New Orleans's bead-strewn Mardi Gras parades, with their extravagant floats and costumes, has often been noted. But the various natural landscapes of her childhood and later choosing are equally important. Most are seaside, among them the island of Kastellorizo in Greece, home to her father's family; East Hampton, on the Eastern Seaboard; and Lake Charles, Louisiana, where she was born and raised, growing up surrounded by water. "The first house my father built for my mother was on stilts," she recalls, "amid rice paddies. I played under the houses, and sometimes went to school in boats." Scuba diving was a longtime passion; she remains an avid swimmer, and aquatic forms—jellyfish, coral—can be seen in her new sculptures. Hence too, perhaps, the impression given by so much of her work that it has been coaxed from fluid matter, starting with the latex pours—which she has compared to oil slicks on the bayou[13]—and including the early foam sculptures and more recent work in clay. Before turning to handmade paper Benglis produced a series of playfully monumental fountains that combine forms originally explored in hand-built clay with cascading water. She confirms a similarity, in some, to the distinctive crawfish "chimneys" that are common to the swampy reaches of south Louisiana.

In notable contrast, the environment of her New Mexico studio, which Benglis has had since

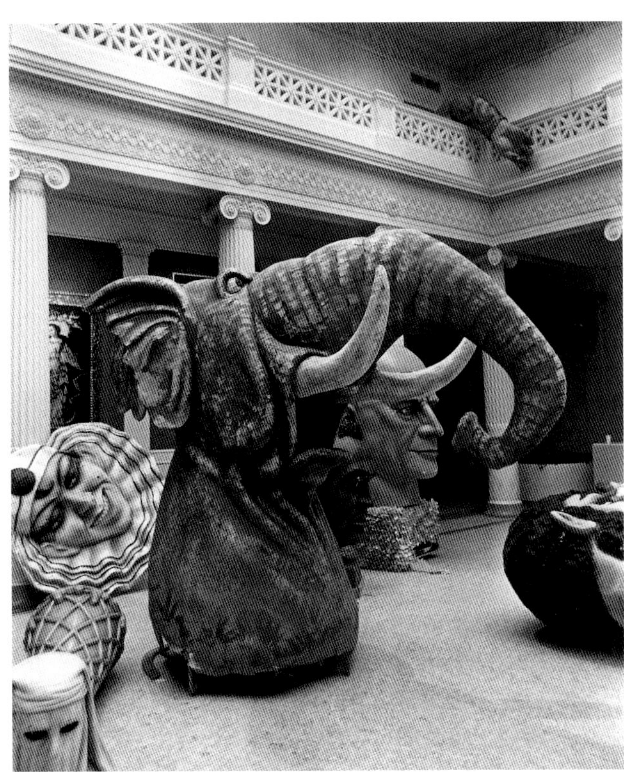

Lynda Benglis and Ida Kohlmeyer, *Louisiana Prop Piece*, 1977, mixed media
New Orleans Museum of Art, 1977

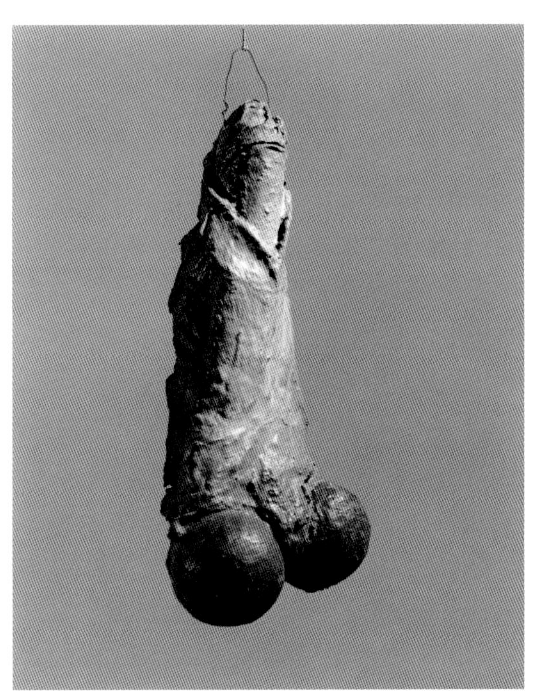

Louise Bourgeois, *Fillette*, 1968, latex over plaster
23 1/2 x 10 1/2 x 7 3/4 in
Collection Museum of Modern Art, New York

1993 and where she has made the paper works, is sere and windblown. It is possible to see the bleached bones of the land—its mesas and arroyos; its scatterings of shed snakeskins and animal skeletons—in the new sculptures' combination of strength and delicacy. Some, like *Torn Totem*, suggest bone freshly scraped and bleached, and haunted by faint traces of flesh. But in answer to the question of what led her to this arid landscape, she exclaims, "There is water in the sky all the time— the most wonderful clouds I've ever seen!" *Storm a' Coming* (plate 32), with its pair of roiling, black-flecked billows closing in on a streak of shining blue, seems to celebrate the local climate's drama. Benglis first visited New Mexico when she was a child, for a family vacation on a horse ranch, and she treasures, as she did then, the remarkable clarity of the area's light and the rugged contours of its sandstone and lava formations, comparing the current work to a rock collection she had as a child. While the new sculptures are not as diminutive as that comparison suggests, they are scaled to the human body; they're smaller than the relatively monumental recent fountains, or the sited sculptures she has made in India. As early as 1970, she sought to counter what she saw as the "big macho game" of Abstract Expressionism and its afterlife in the Minimalist sculpture and even the video art of the seventies.[14] Describing the new works as a kind of portrait gallery, Benglis says each has its own personality and, quoting Picasso, enlists them in a pas de deux of seduction. "They look back at you," she says. "I'm involved with romancing them."

In "Every Force Evolves a Form," the essayist Guy Davenport considers the many roles of birds in culture and metaphor. Proceeding from Emily Dickinson's lark to Wordsworth's robin, Poe's raven, Whitman's osprey and Gerard Manley Hopkins's falcon, Davenport writes, "The history of birds taken to be *daimons* traverses religion, folklore, and literature"; he concludes by calling the poets' many winged creatures "a dance of forms to a perennial spiritual force." Benglis's new work, similarly flight-bound, and propelled by forces at once sensual and humane, is also, as she describes it, a sustained and sustaining dance.

[1] Interview with Robert James Coad, 1988, cited in Susan Krane, "Lynda Benglis: Theatres of Nature," in *Lynda Benglis: Dual Natures* (Atlanta: High Museum of Art, 1990), 21.

[2] Coad, in Krane, 27.

[3] Conversation with the author, June 10, 2016. Unless otherwise noted, quotes of the artist are from this conversation.

[4] Rene Ricard, "New York: Lynda Benglis at Paula Cooper," *Art in America*, January/February 1979, 141.

[5] "Interview: Lynda Benglis," *Ocular* 32, cited in Krane, 41.

[6] See, for instance, Elisabeth Lebovici, "Lynda Benglis: All That Matters . . ." in Franck Gautherot, Caroline Hancock and Seungduk Kim, editors, *Lynda Benglis* (Dijon: les presses du réel, 2009), 85, and Susan Richmond, *Lynda Benglis: Beyond Process* (London and New York: I.B. Tauris, 2013), 122–23. Among the (characteristically) heterogeneous list of qualities Sontag attributed to camp, those that seem relevant—to the love of Lucy and/or the work of Benglis—are its androgyny and extravagance, and that "Behind the 'straight' public sense in which something can be taken, one has found a private zany experience of the thing." Susan Sontag, "Notes on 'Camp,'" *Against Interpretation and Other Essays* (New York and London: Anchor Books, 1990).

[7] Lucy Kumara Moore, conversation with Lynda Benglis, *Marfa Journal*, no. 5, 2016: 312.

[8] Quoted in Robert Pincus-Witten, "Lynda Benglis: The Frozen Gesture," *Artforum* 13, no. 13 November 1974: 54.

[9] T. J. Clark, *Farewell to an Idea: Episodes from a History of Modernism* (New Haven and London: Yale University Press, 1999), 335.

[10] In the *Knots* that followed, another connection to Pollock has been seen: Jeremy Gilbert-Rolfe, observing that the tubular forms of the *Knots* derived from the circumference of Benglis's arm, said this origin "seems, at some level, reminiscent of the inevitable references to Pollock's arm that his paintings of the 1947–51 period contain." Jeremy Gilbert-Rolfe, "Reviews: Lynda Benglis, The Clocktower," *Artforum 12*, no. 6, March 1974: 69–70, reprinted in Richard Armstrong and Richard Marshall, *The New Sculpture 1965–75* (New York, Whitney Museum of American Art, 1990), 315. A further connection to Pollock can be seen in the current paper work; early on, Benglis had heard about the organic, painted papier-mâché sculptures Pollock made in circa 1951, which remain little known. See Krane, 27.

[11] Krane, 33.

[12] Again, Clark's observations of Pollock are relevant: "Sex for Pollock most often was splitting and merging and rending and tearing," he writes. And while literal attributions of phallic or vaginal imagery seem "ludicrous" to Clark, he admits that "it is plain as day that sex is the driving force in the earlier paintings" and that "No one in her right mind would want to deny that Pollock's drip paintings are implicated in a whole metaphorics of masculinity." Clark, 356. Arguably, a connection can be made to the pansexuality of Benglis's vocabulary, leery though she is of both Pollock's truculent masculinity and any attributions to her own work of literal female imagery.

[13] M. H. Miller, "The Shape Shifter: How Lynda Benglis Left the Bayou and Messed with the Establishment," *Art News*, Spring 2016.

[14] Quoted in Pincus-Witten, 58.

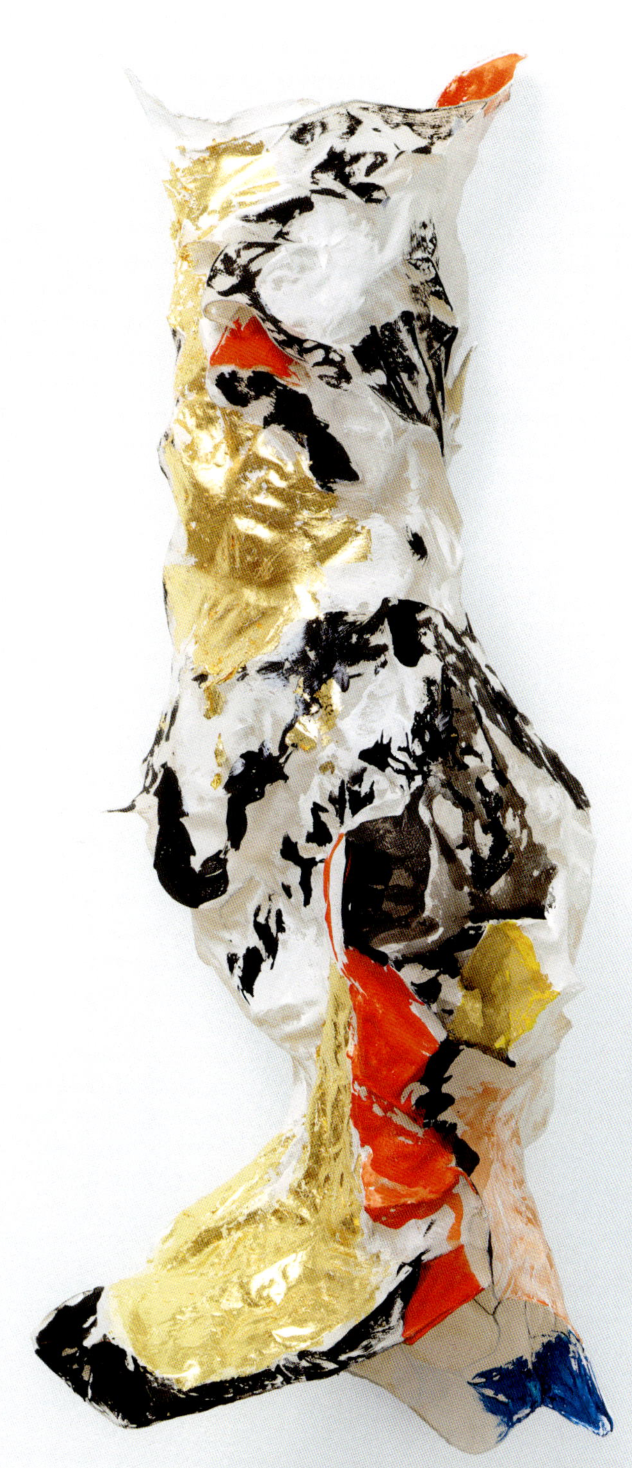

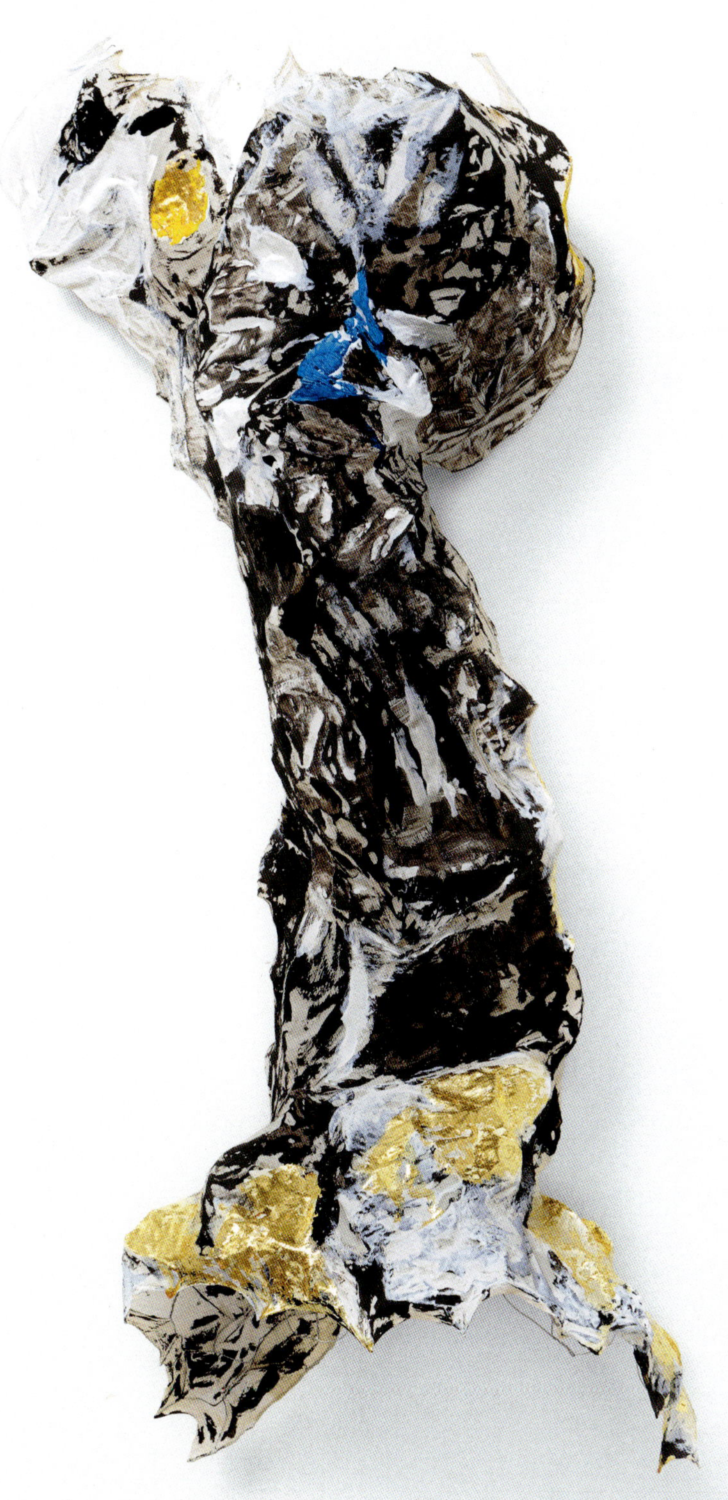

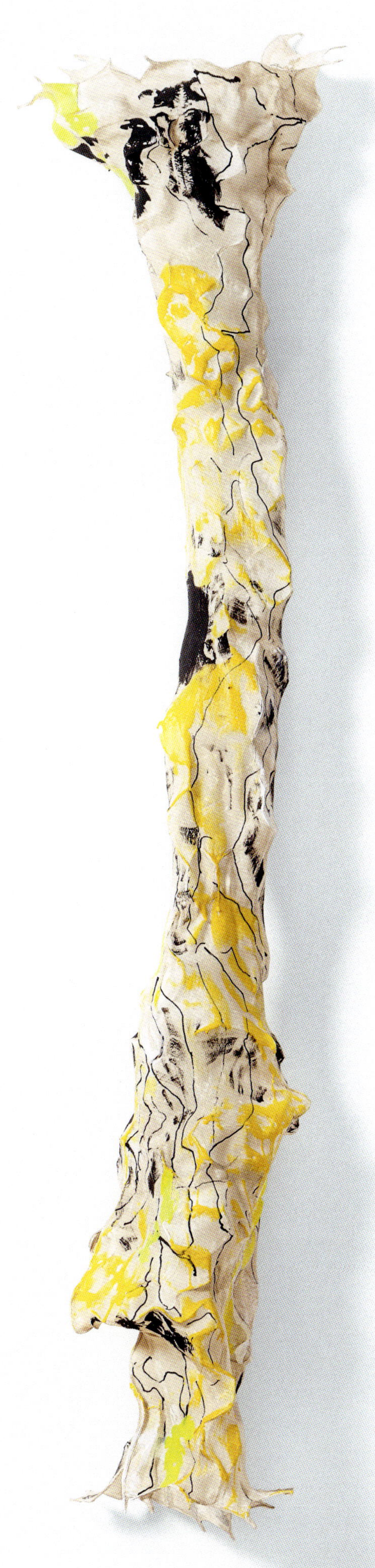

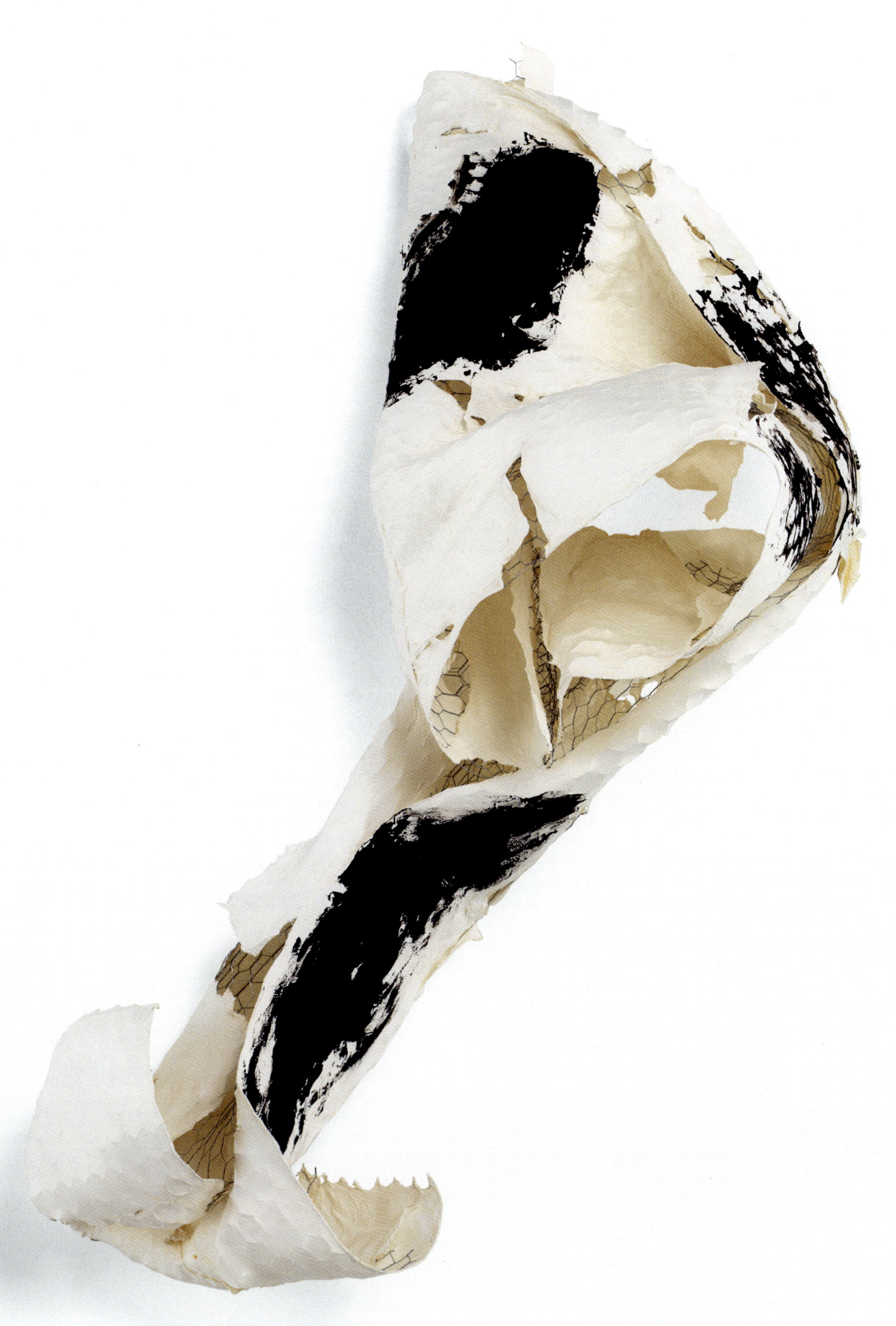

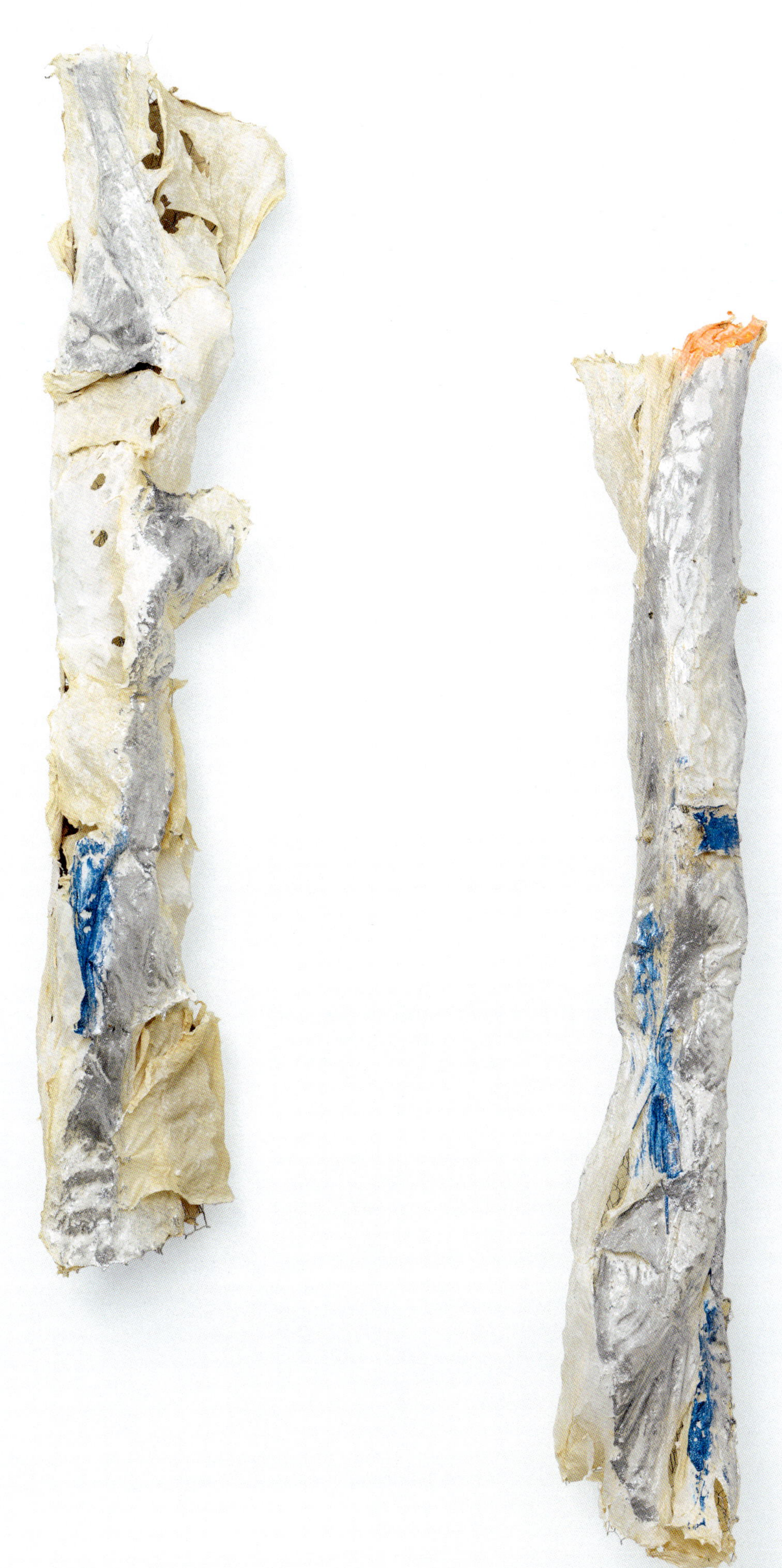

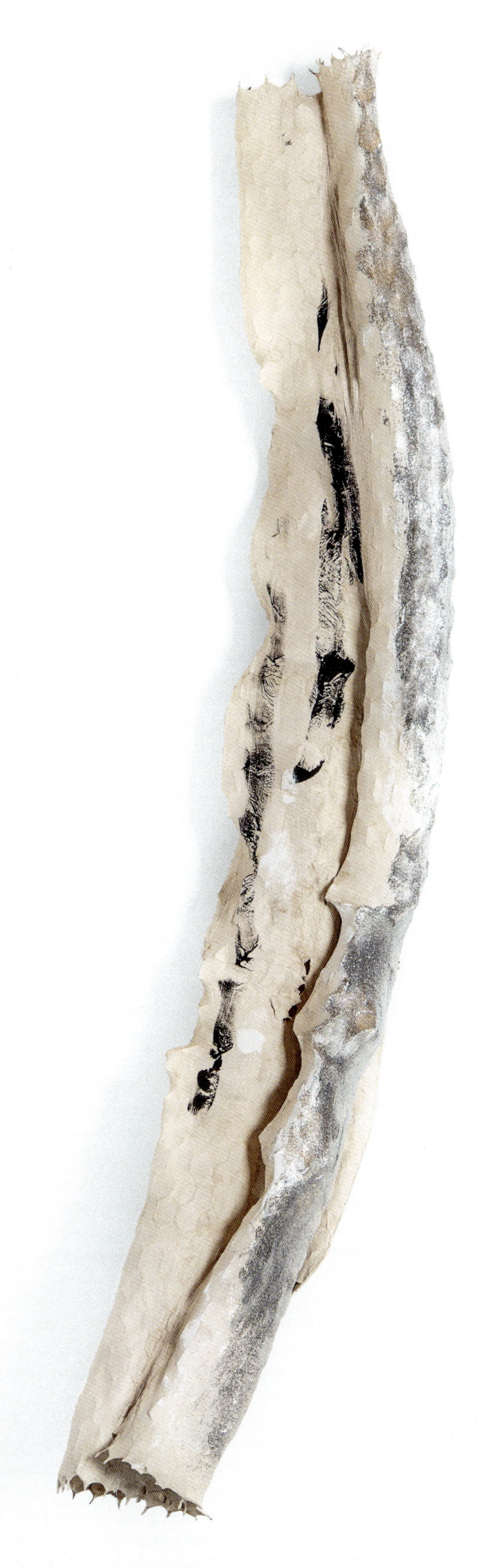

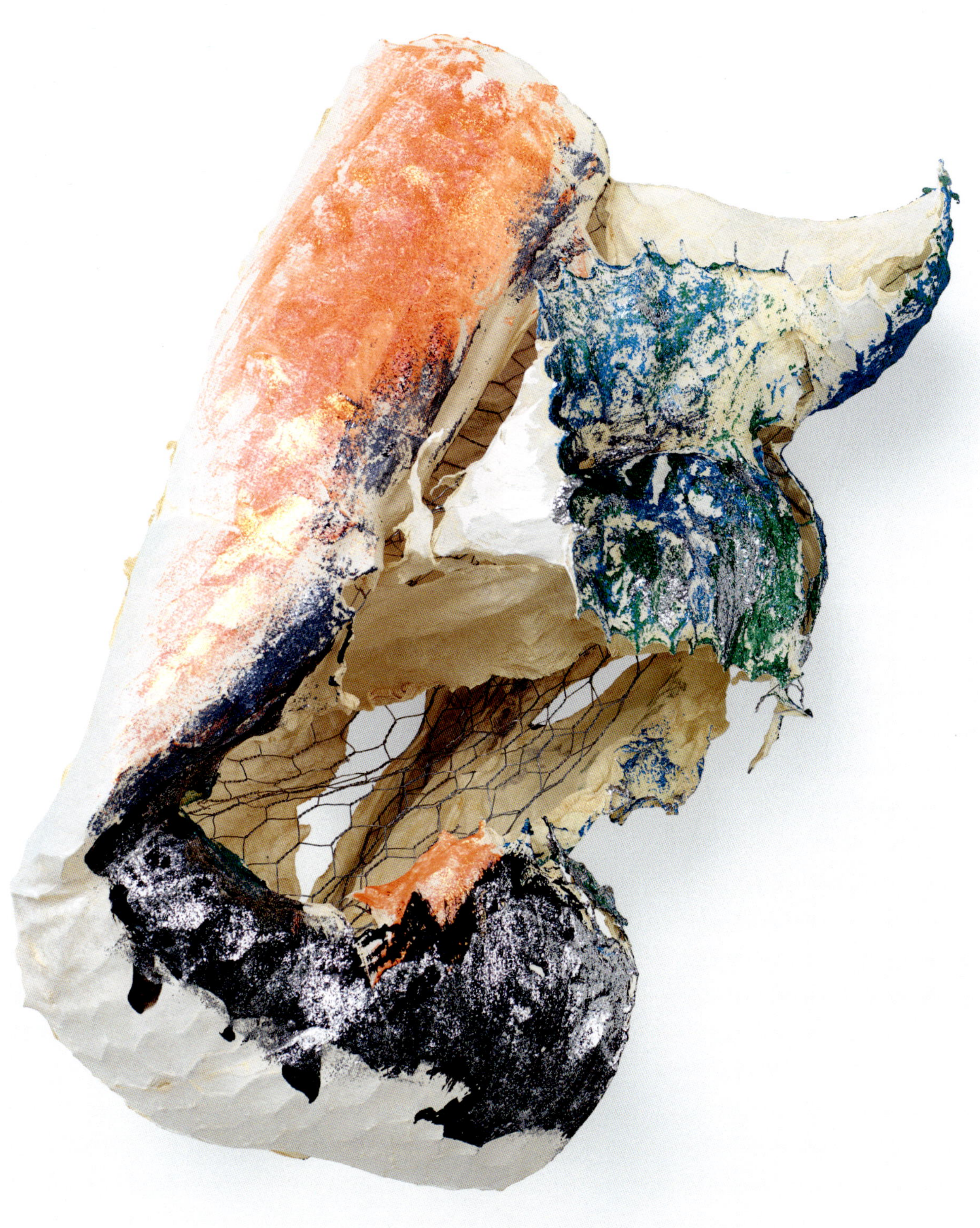

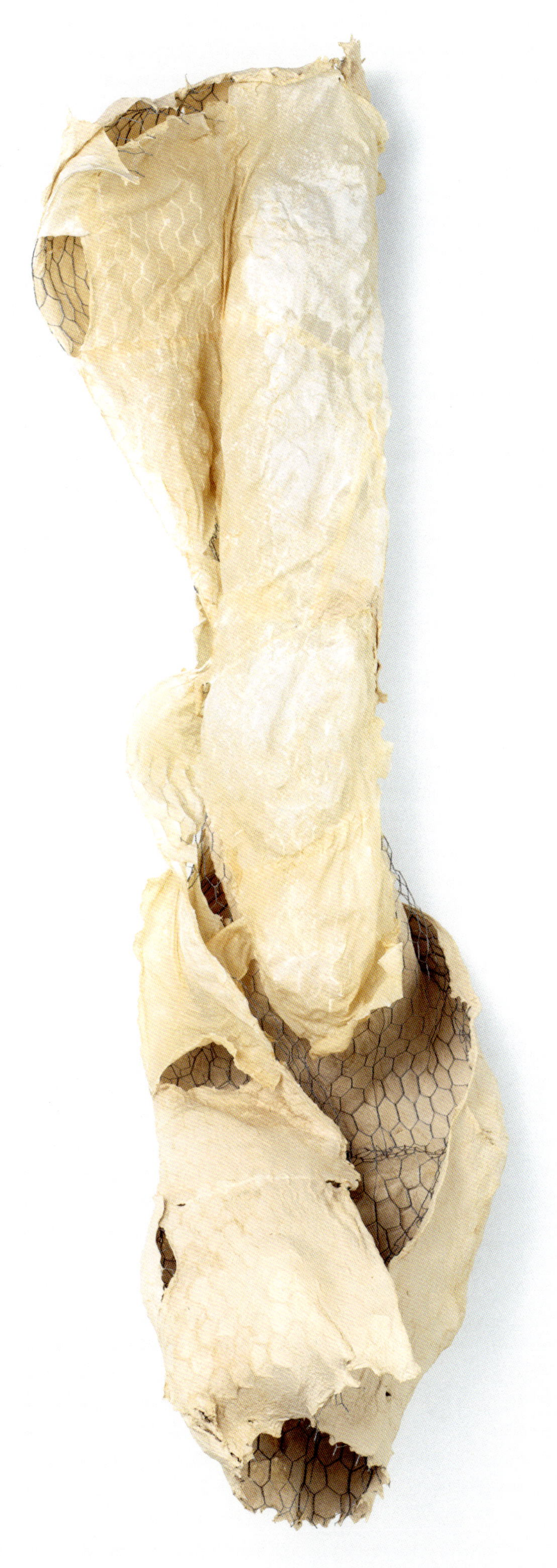

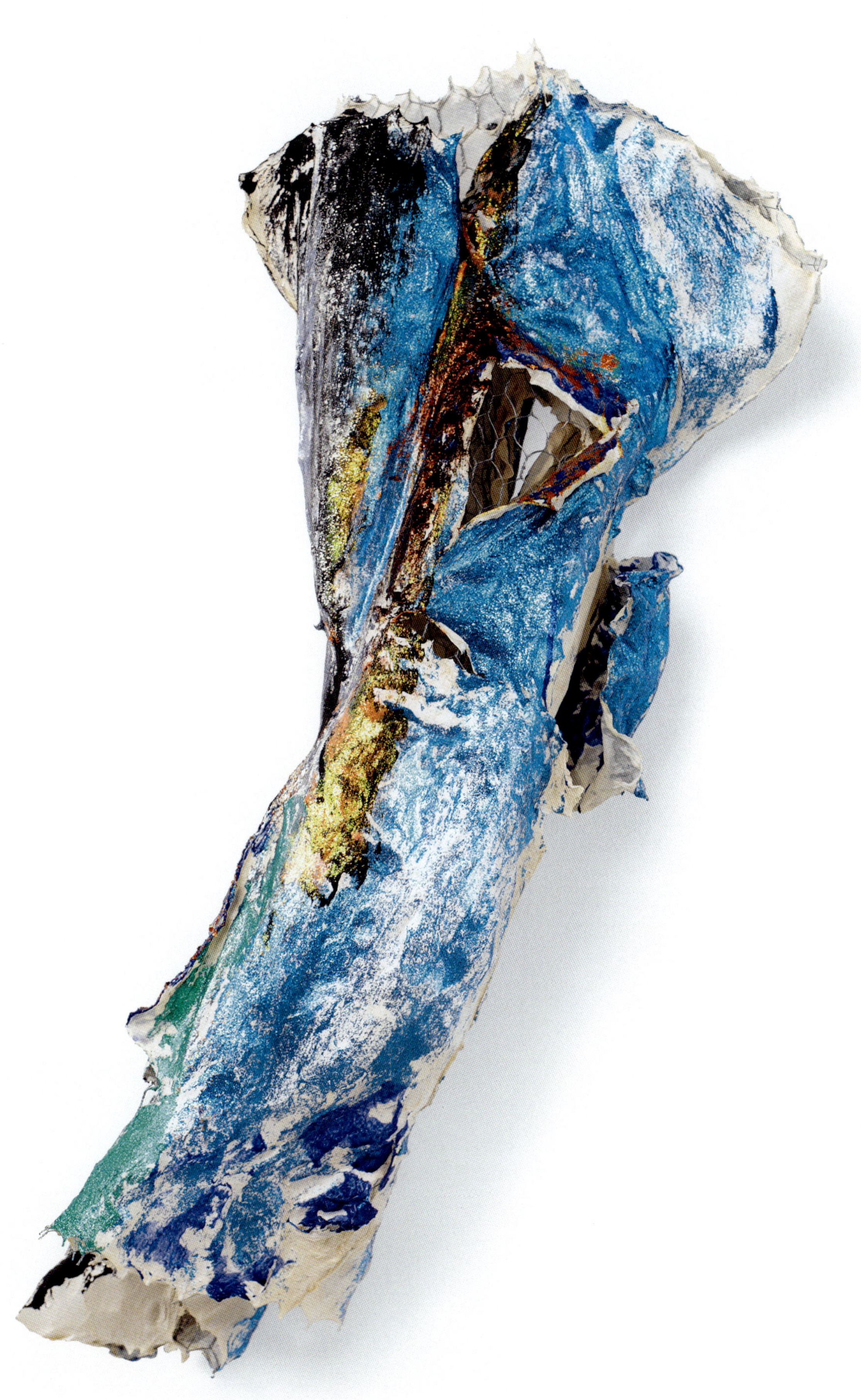

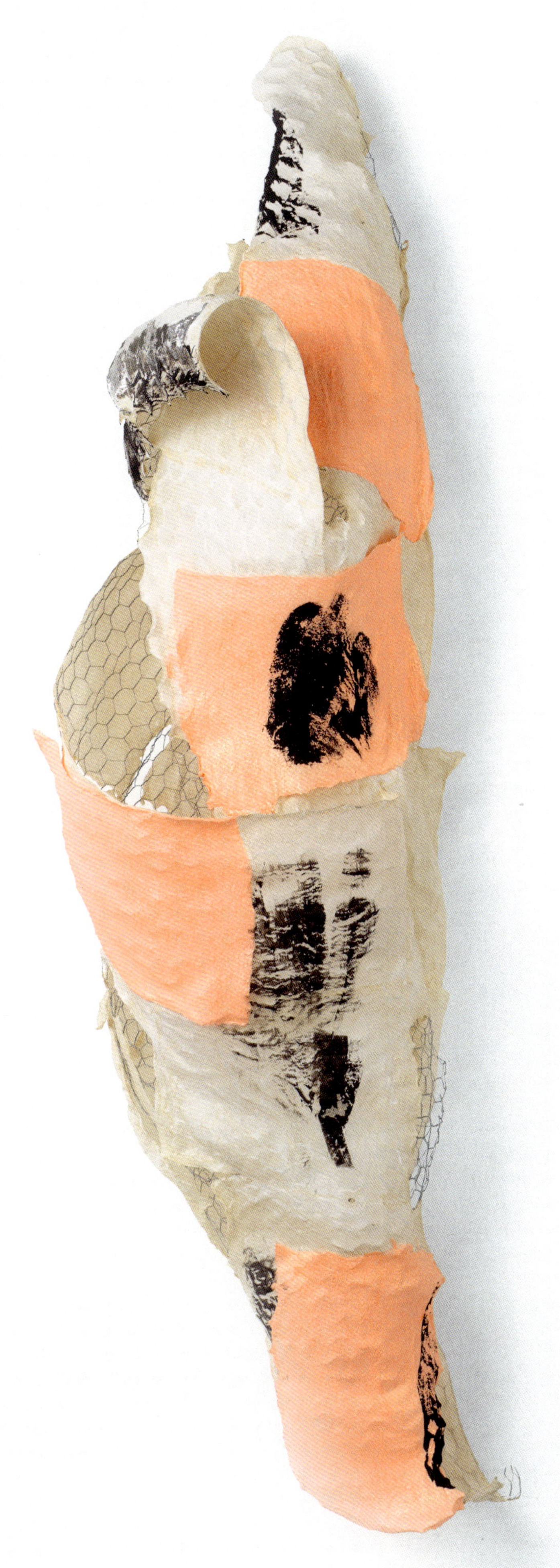

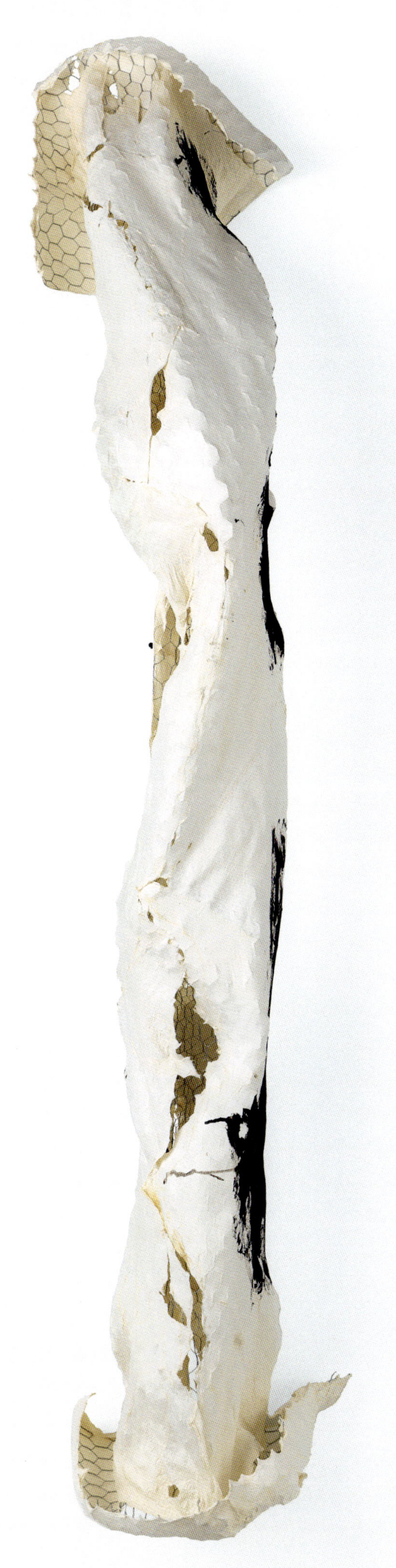

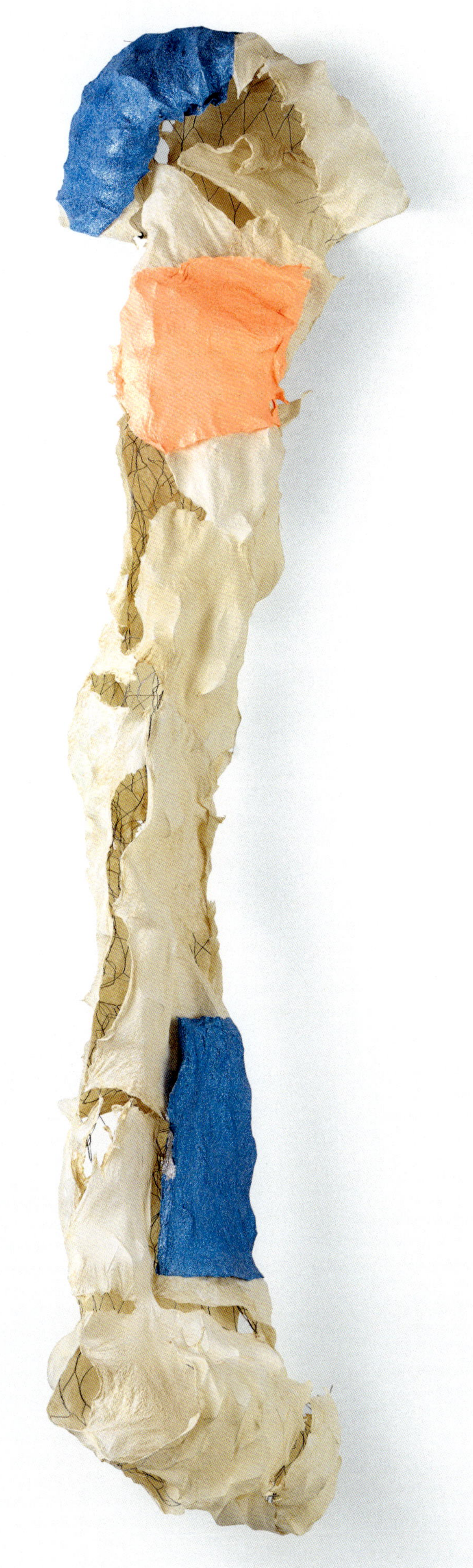

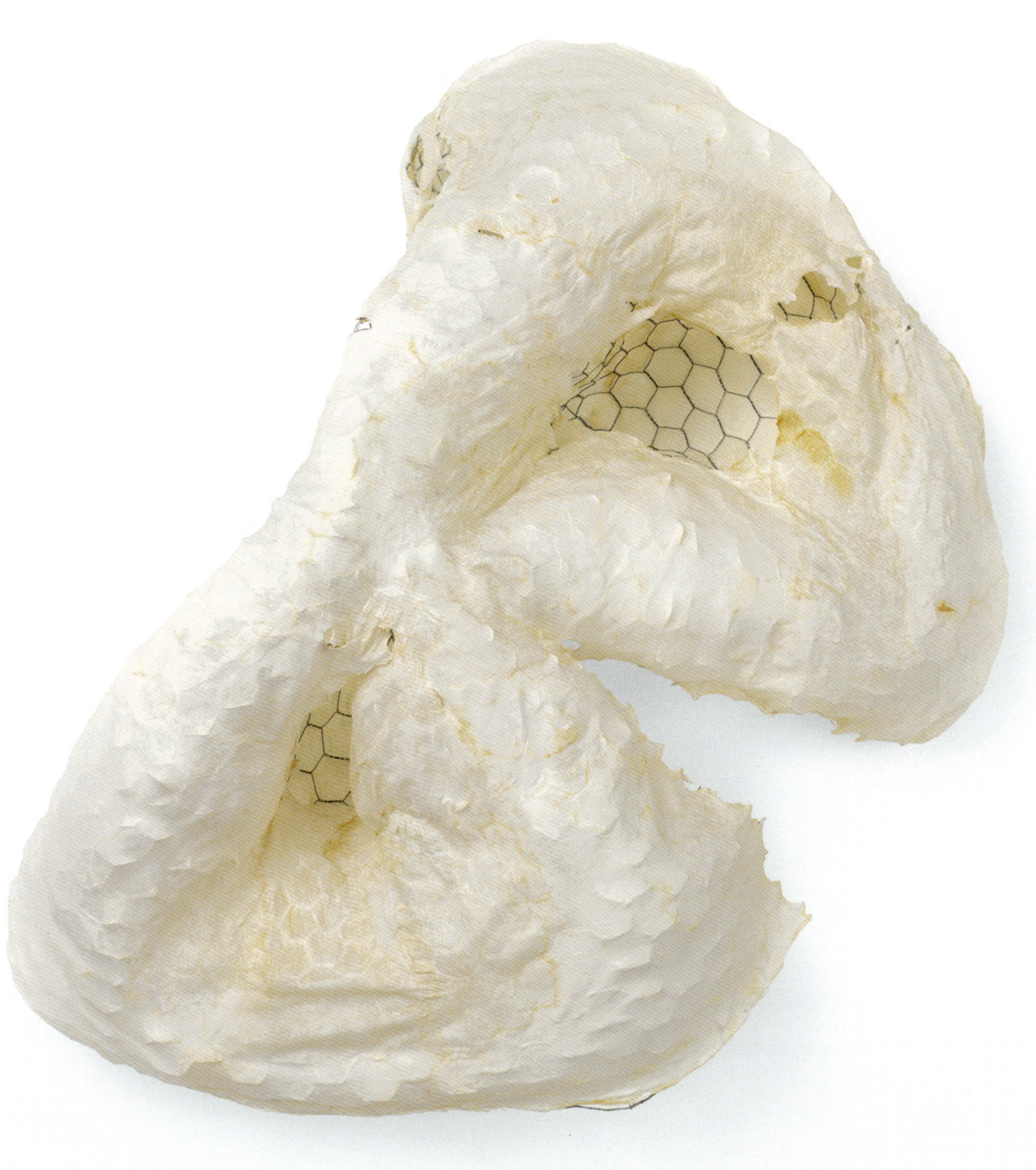

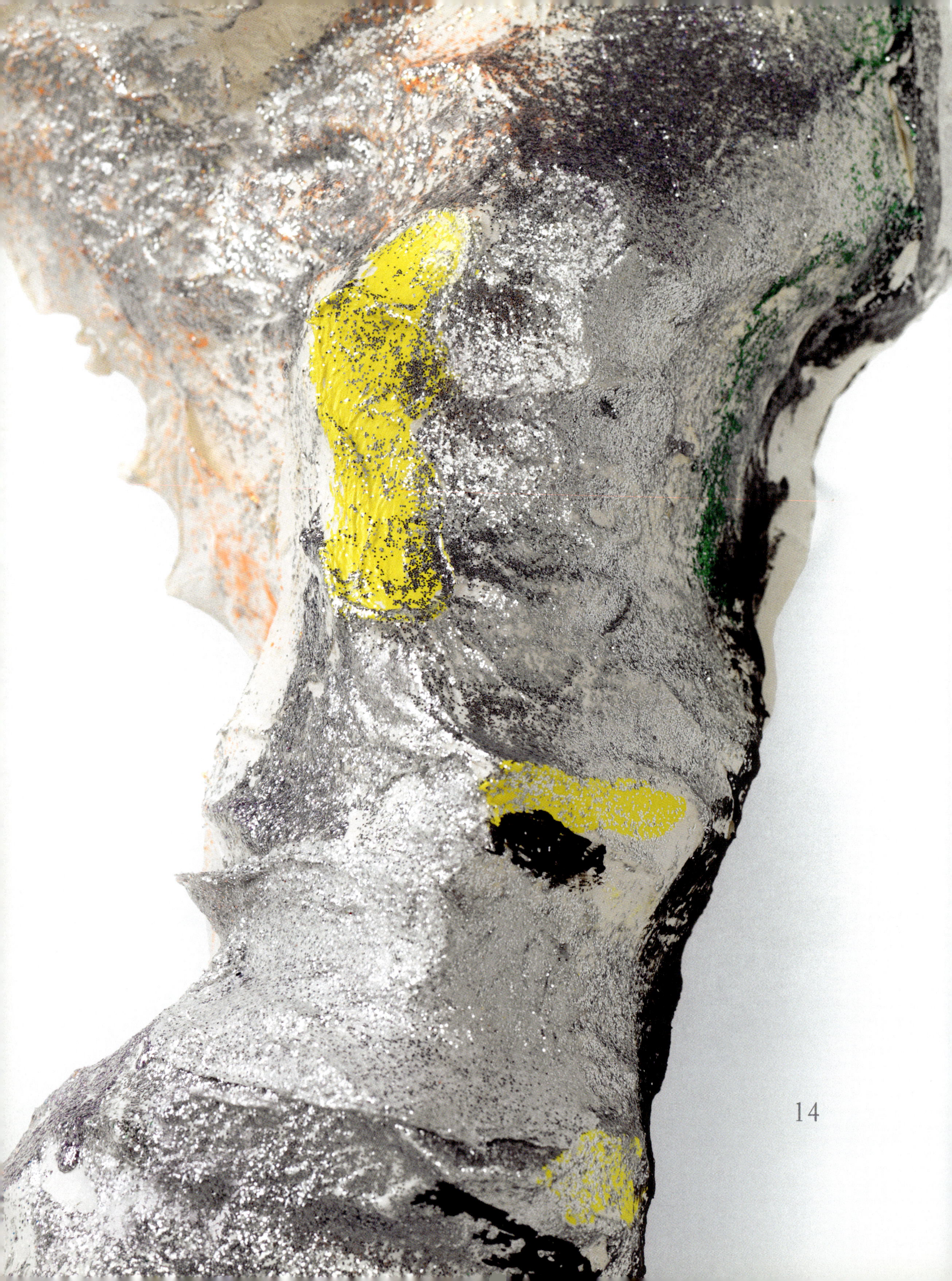

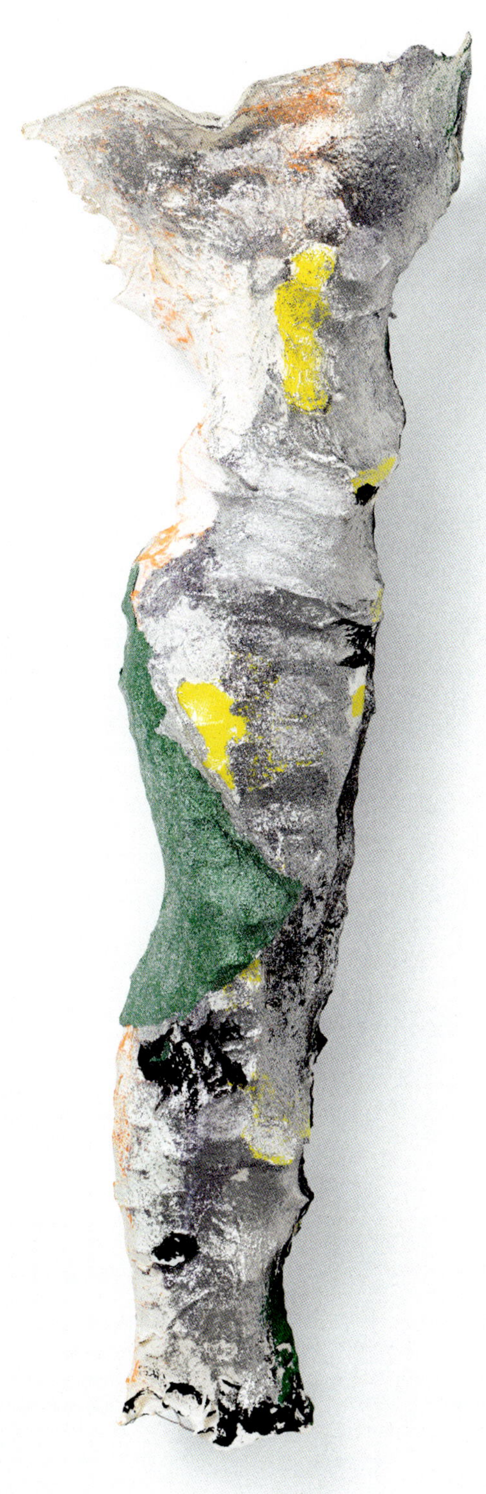

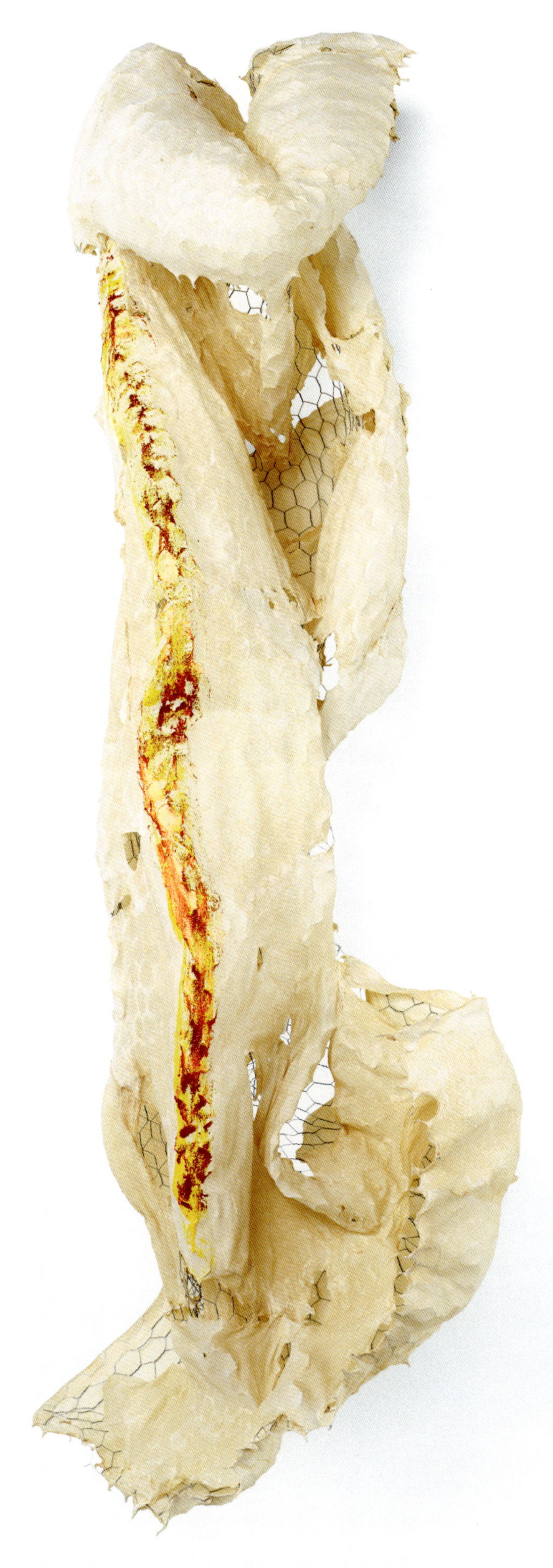

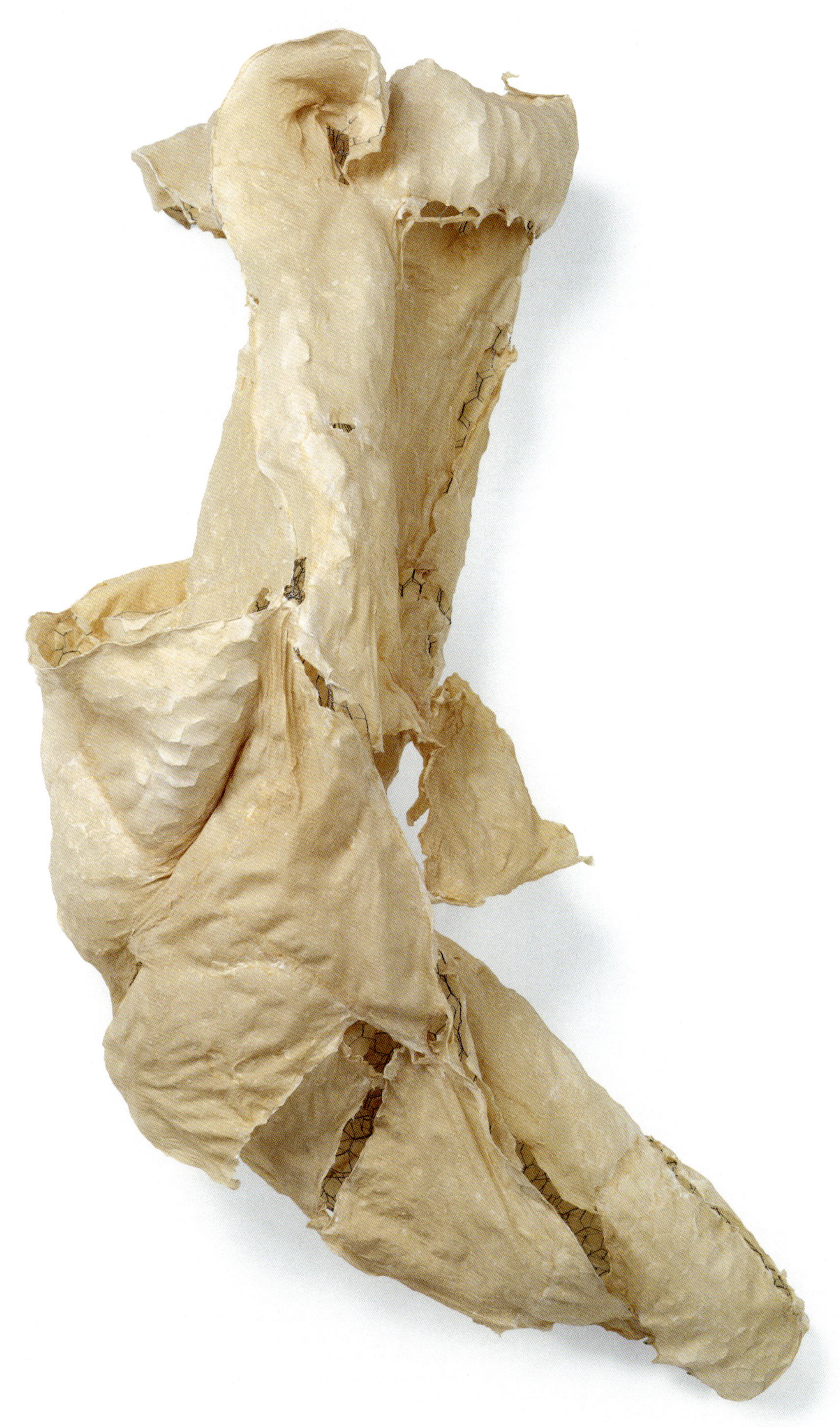

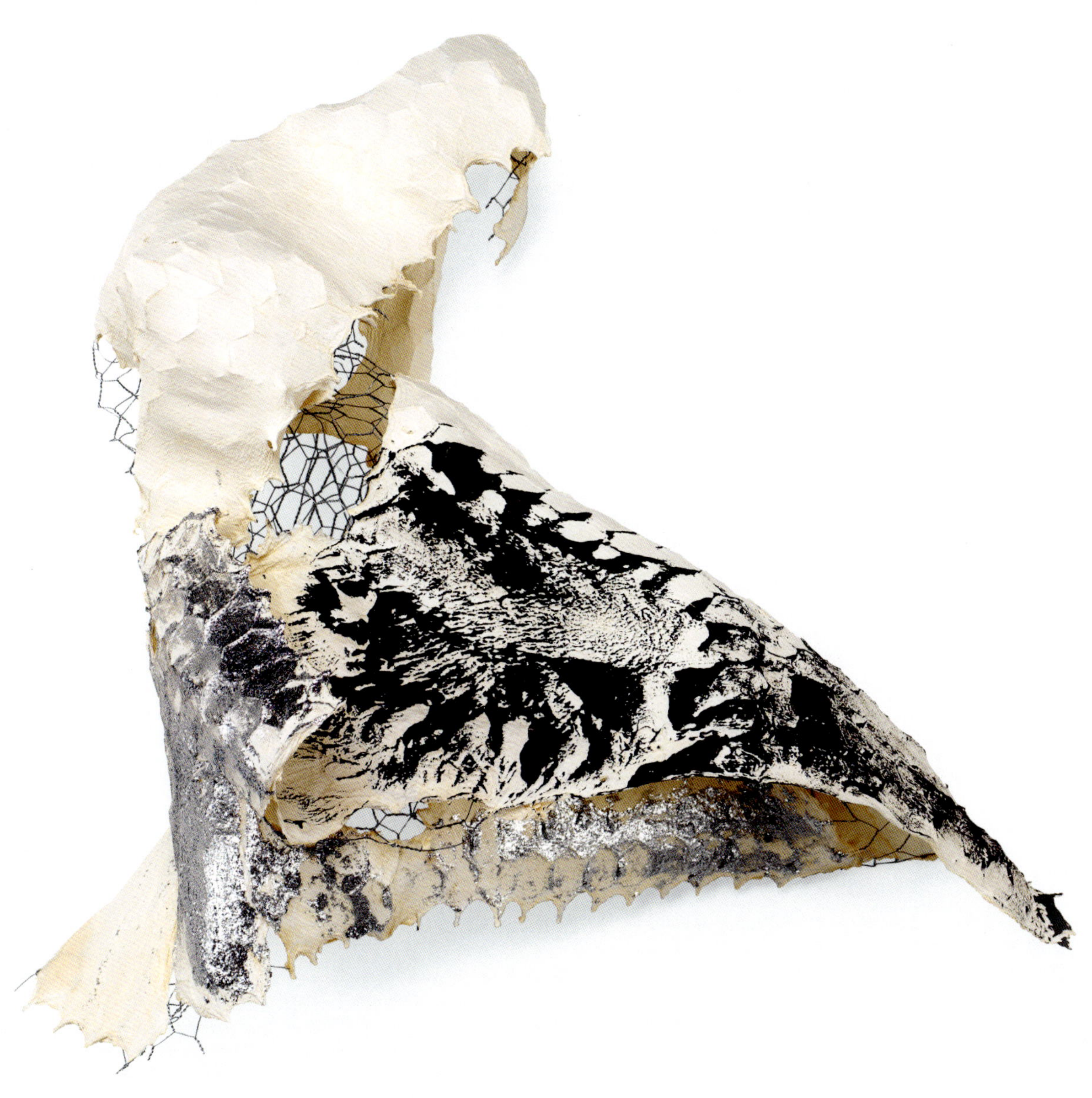

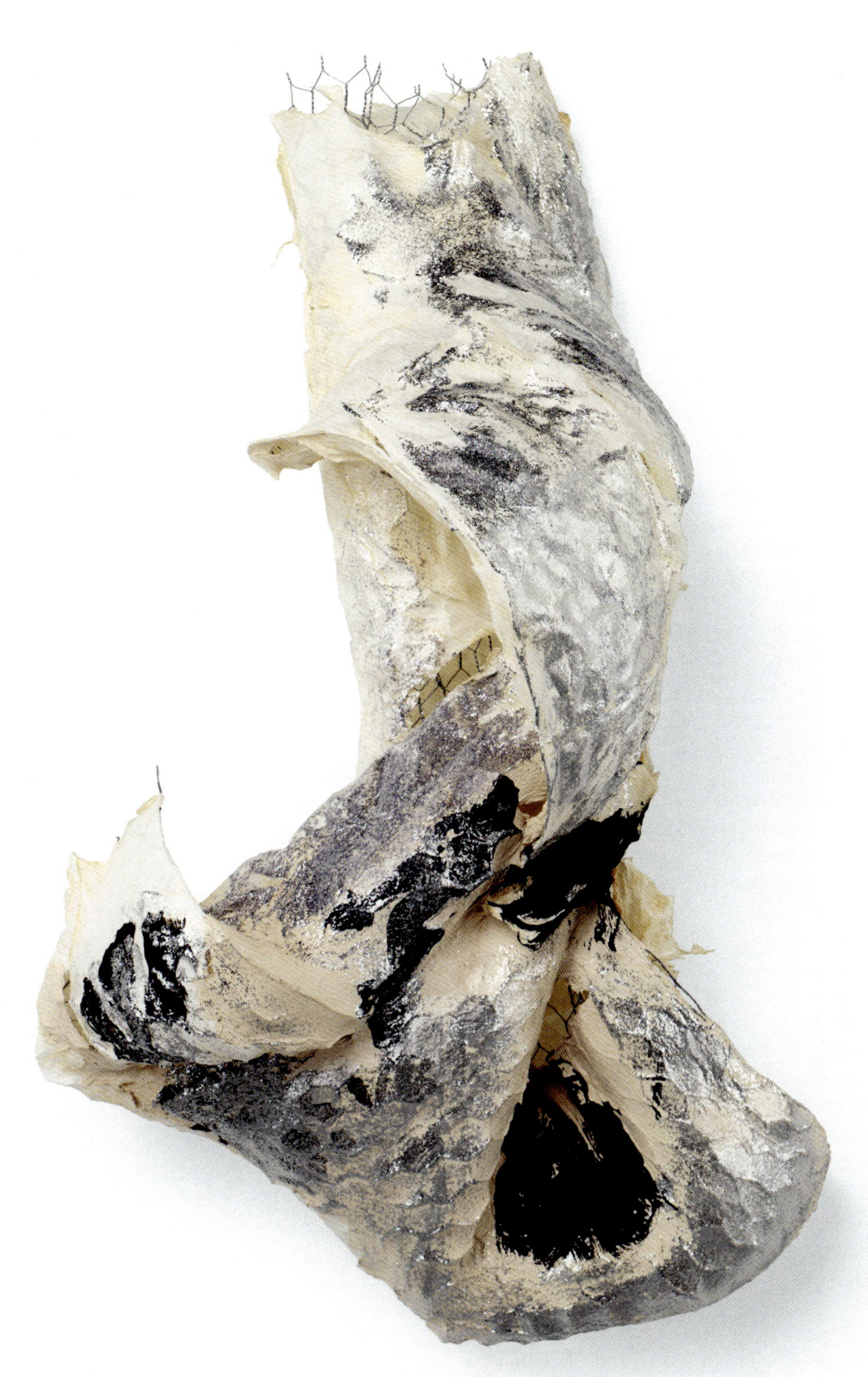

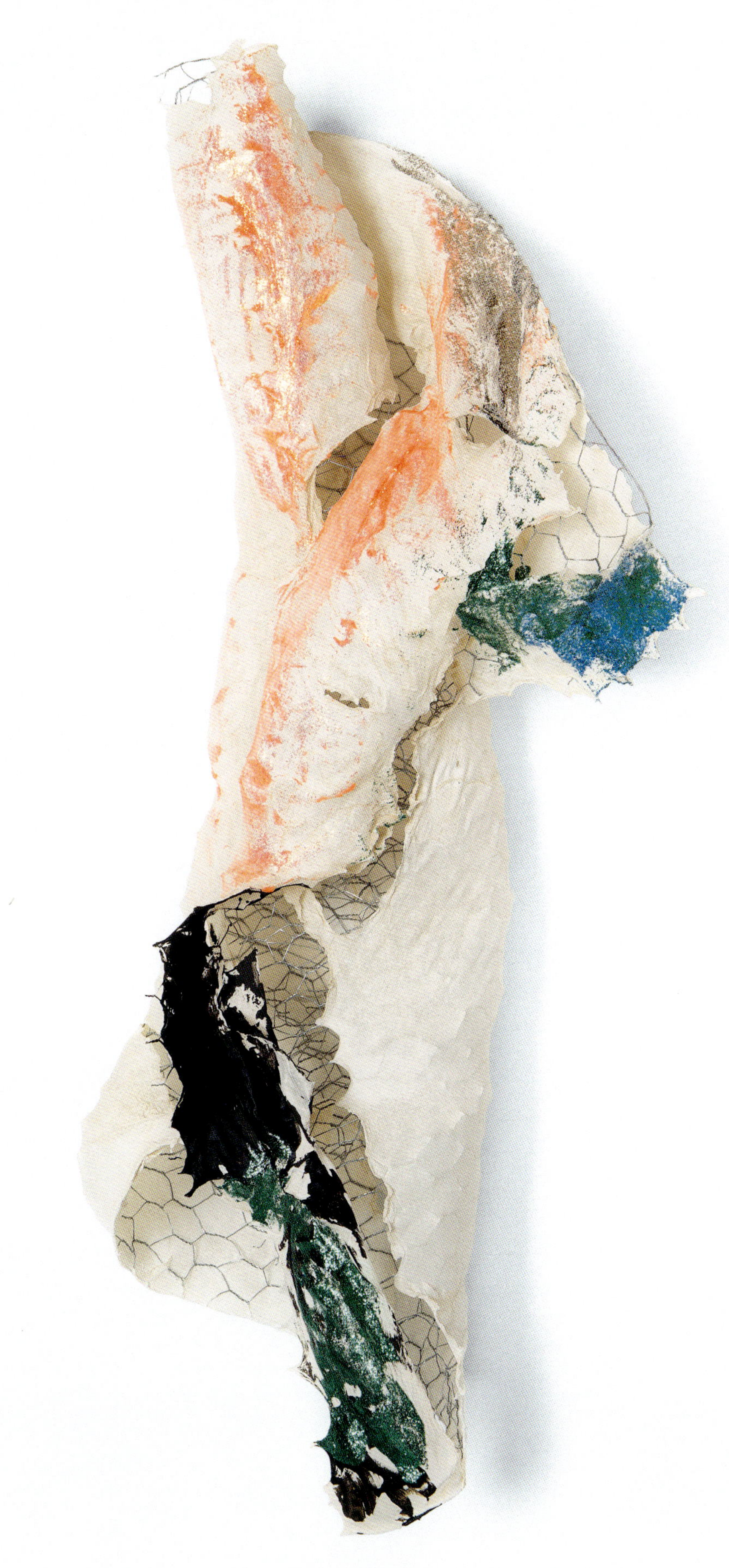

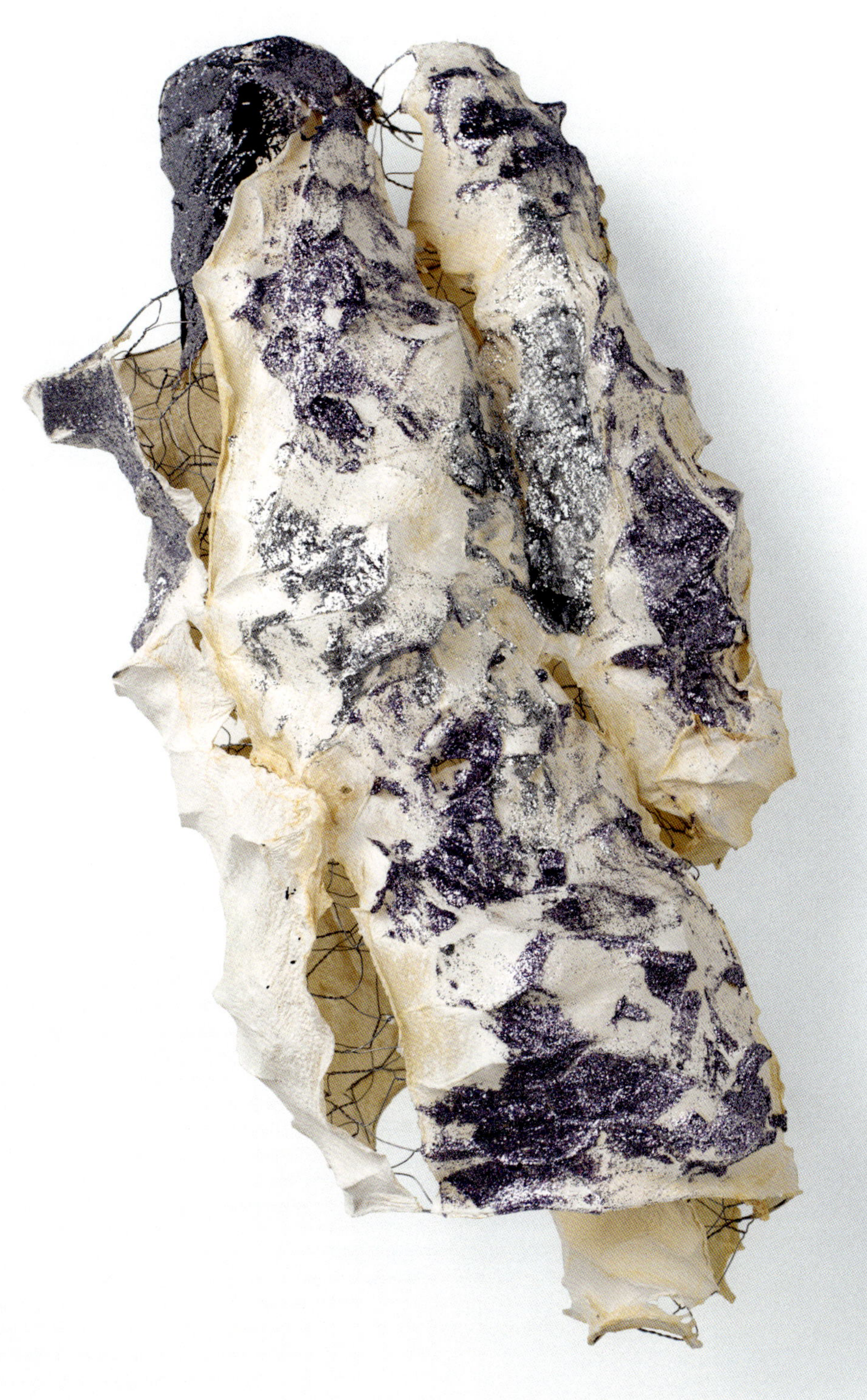

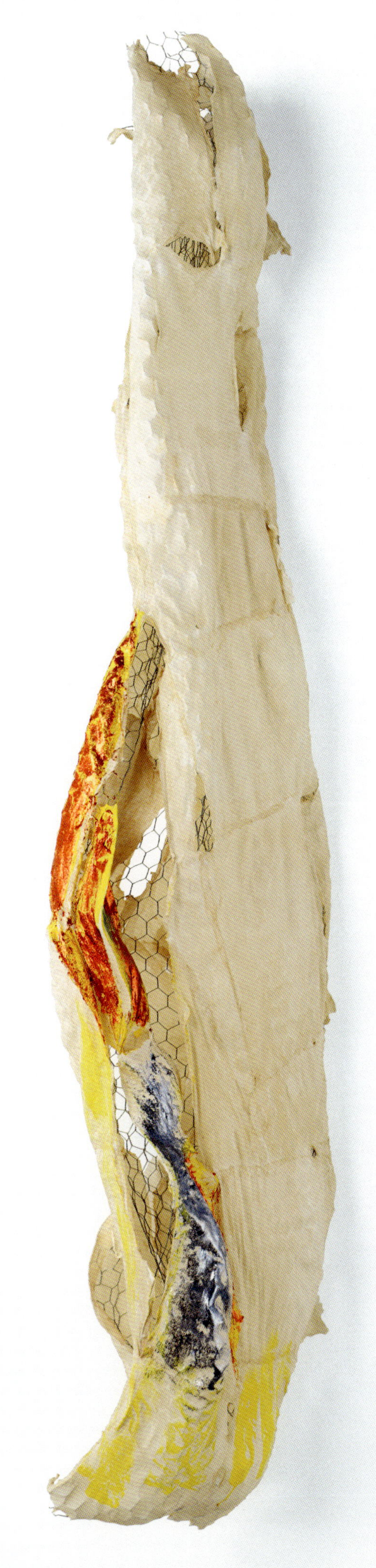

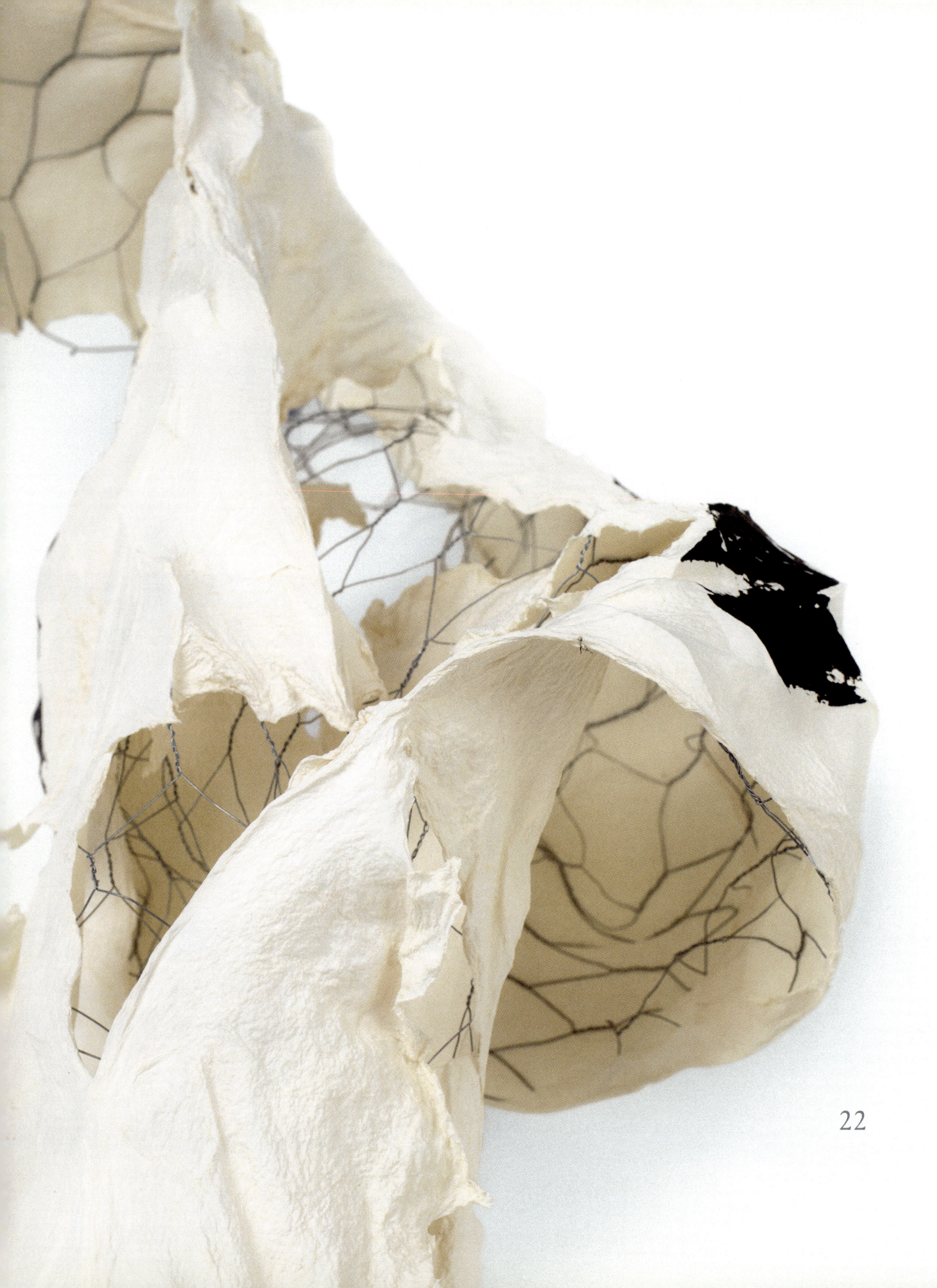

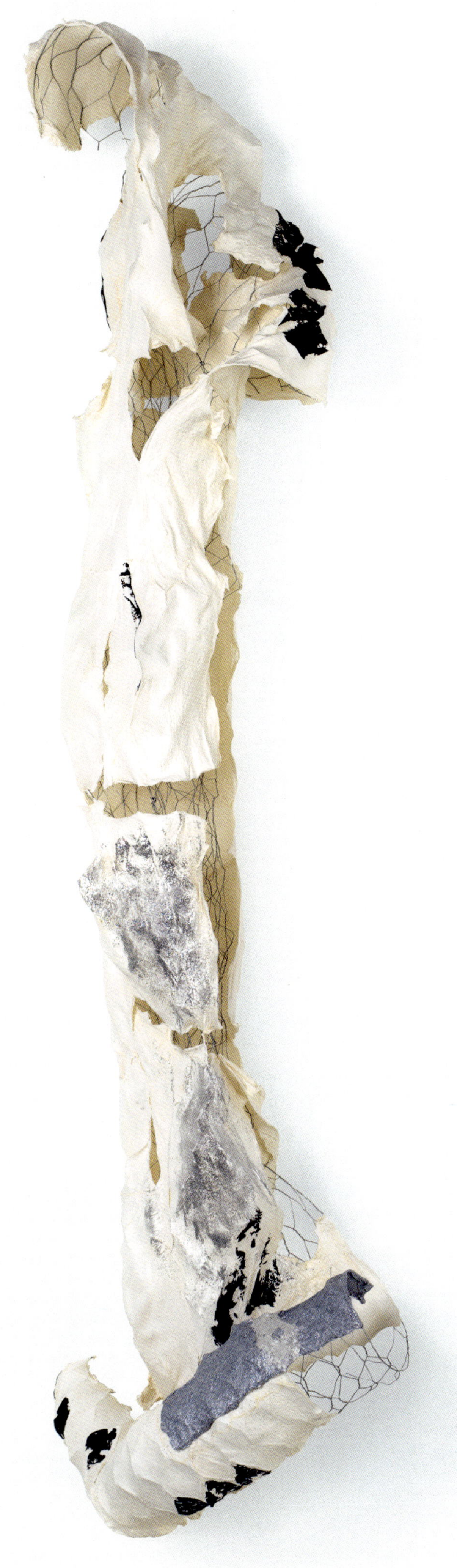

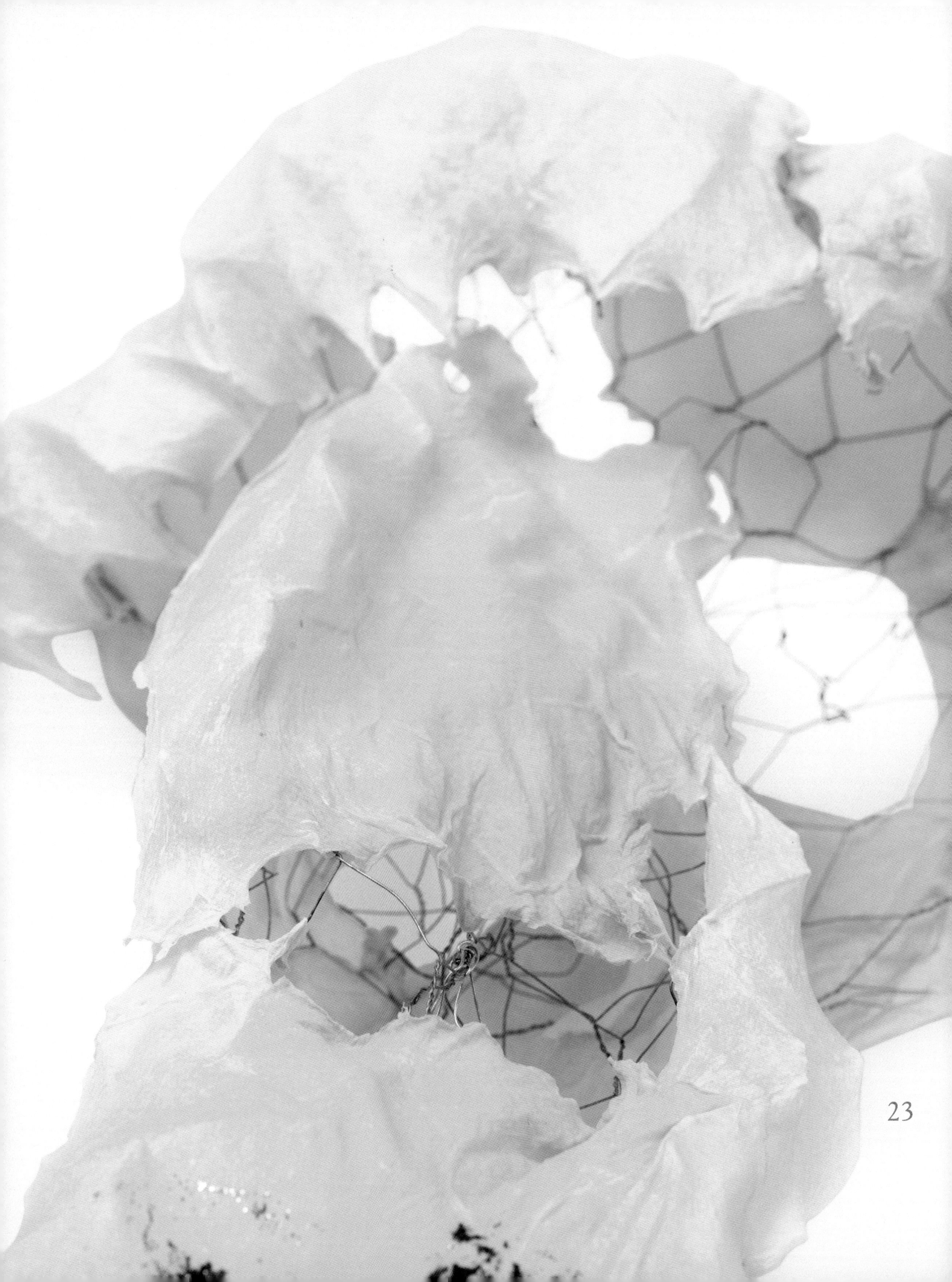

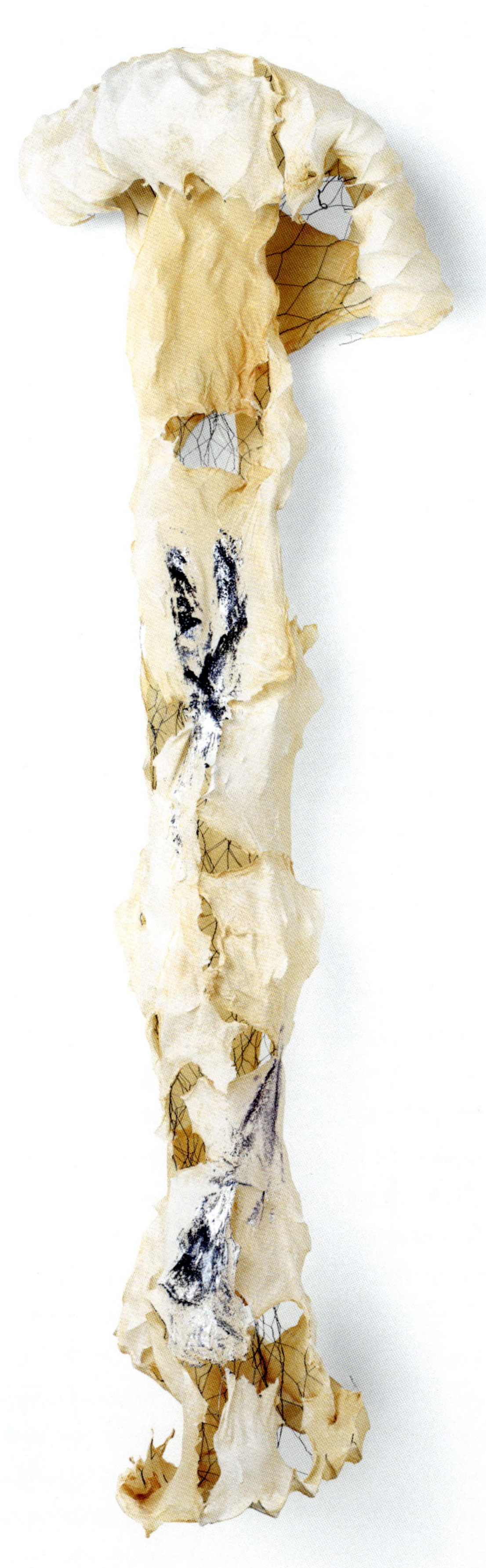

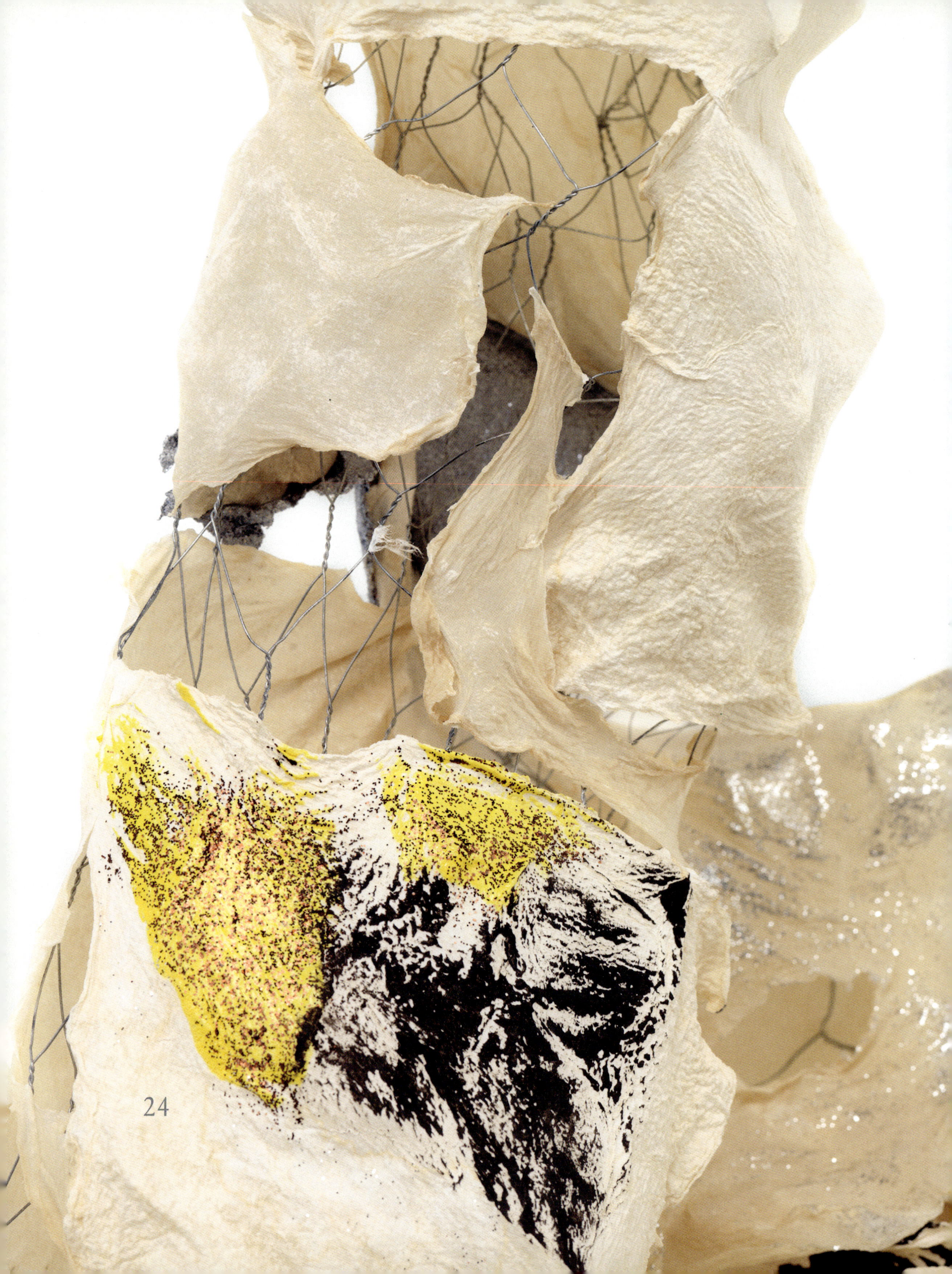

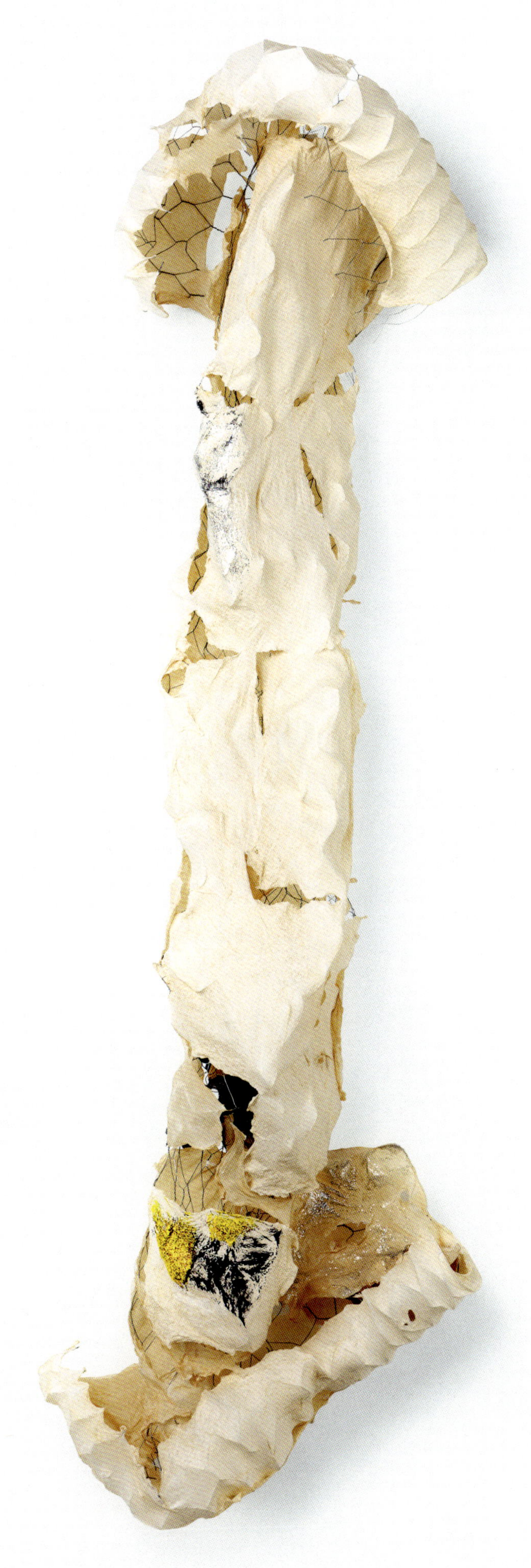

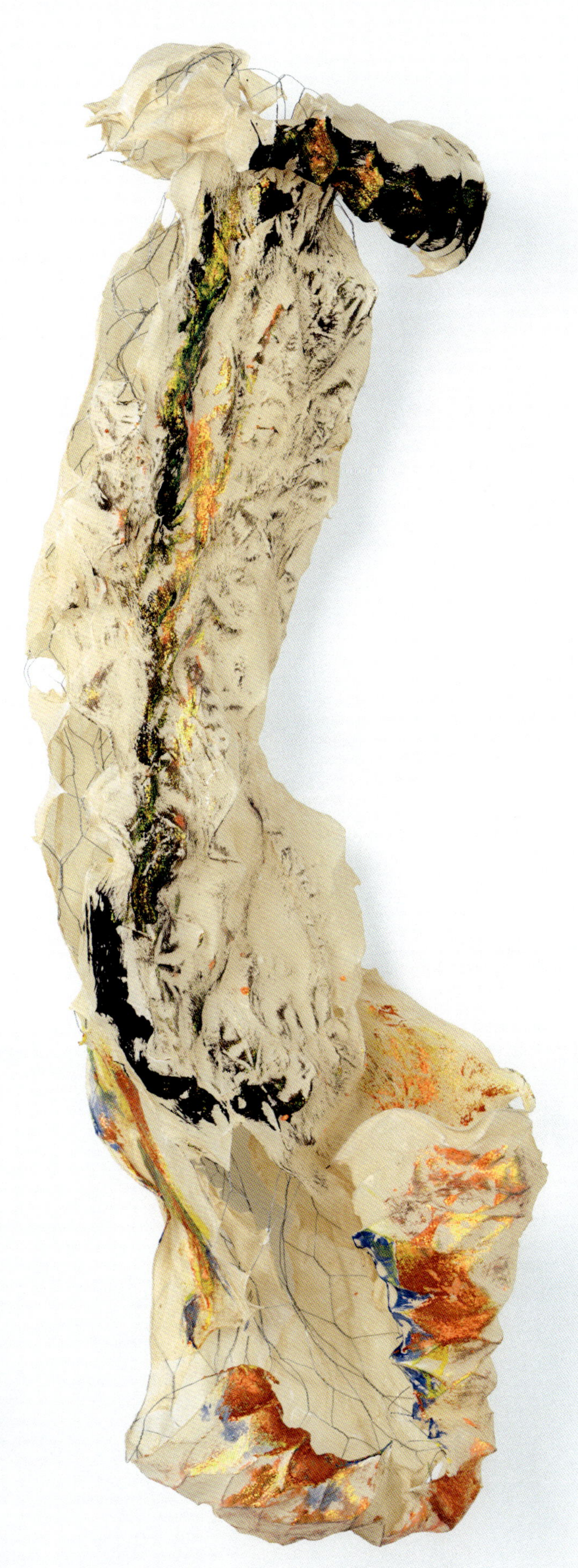

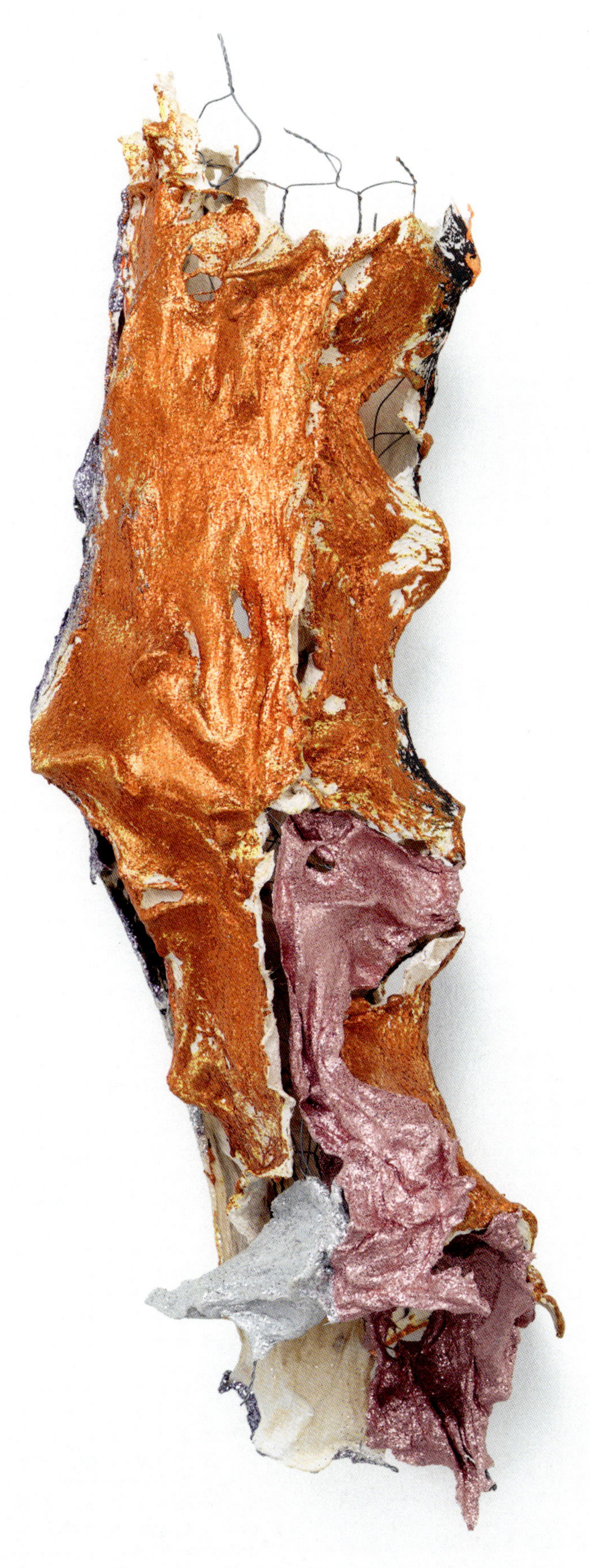

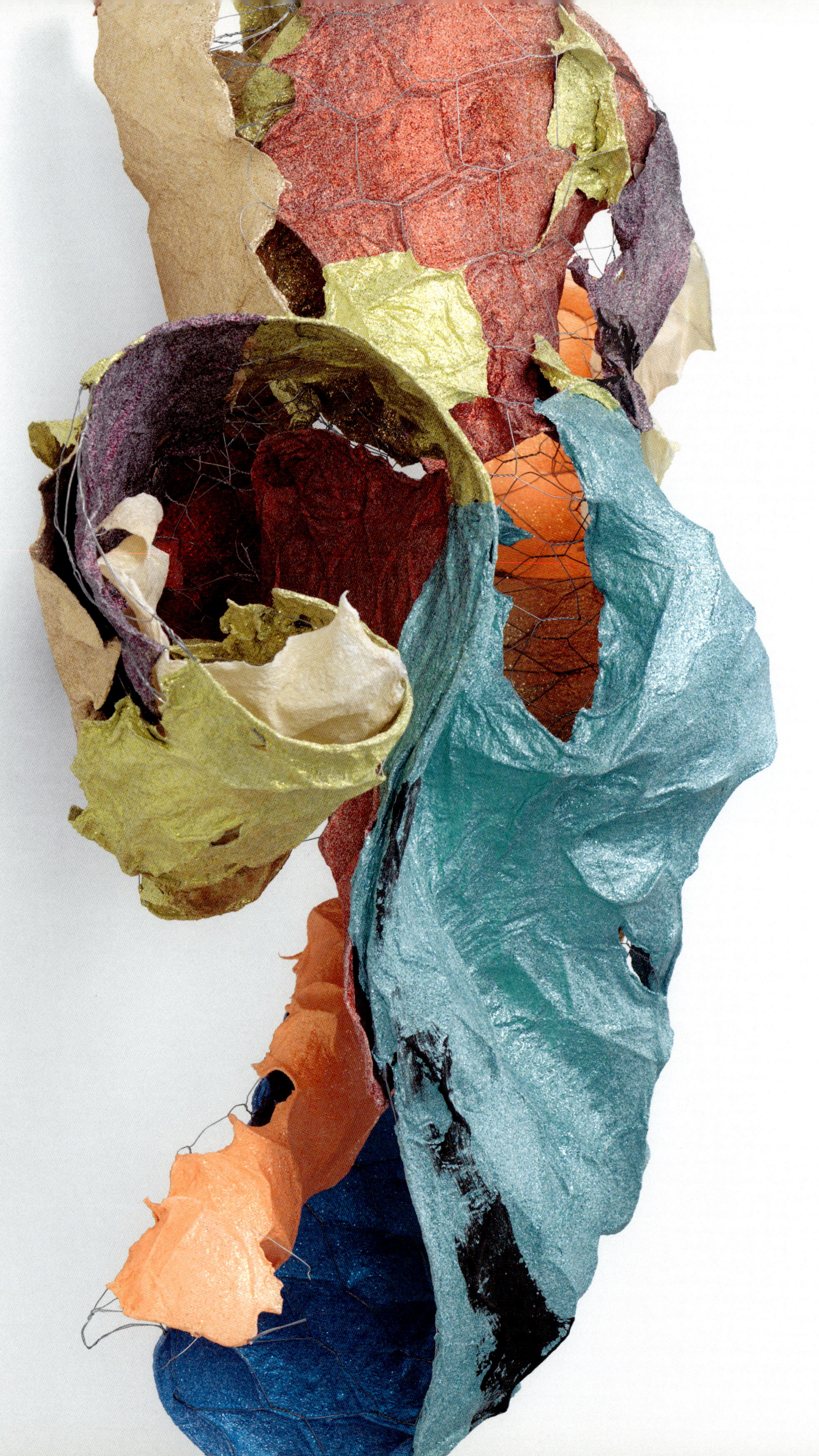

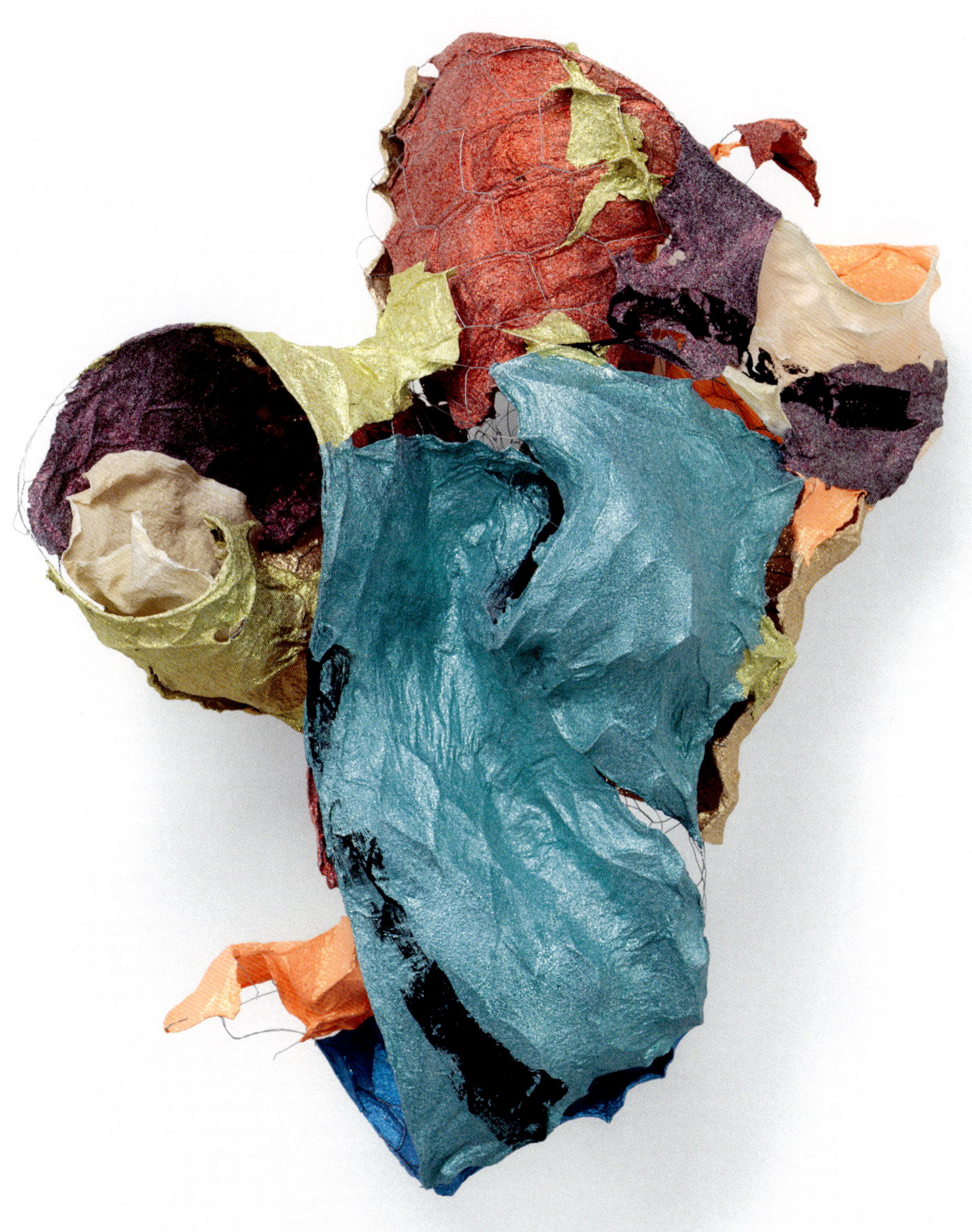

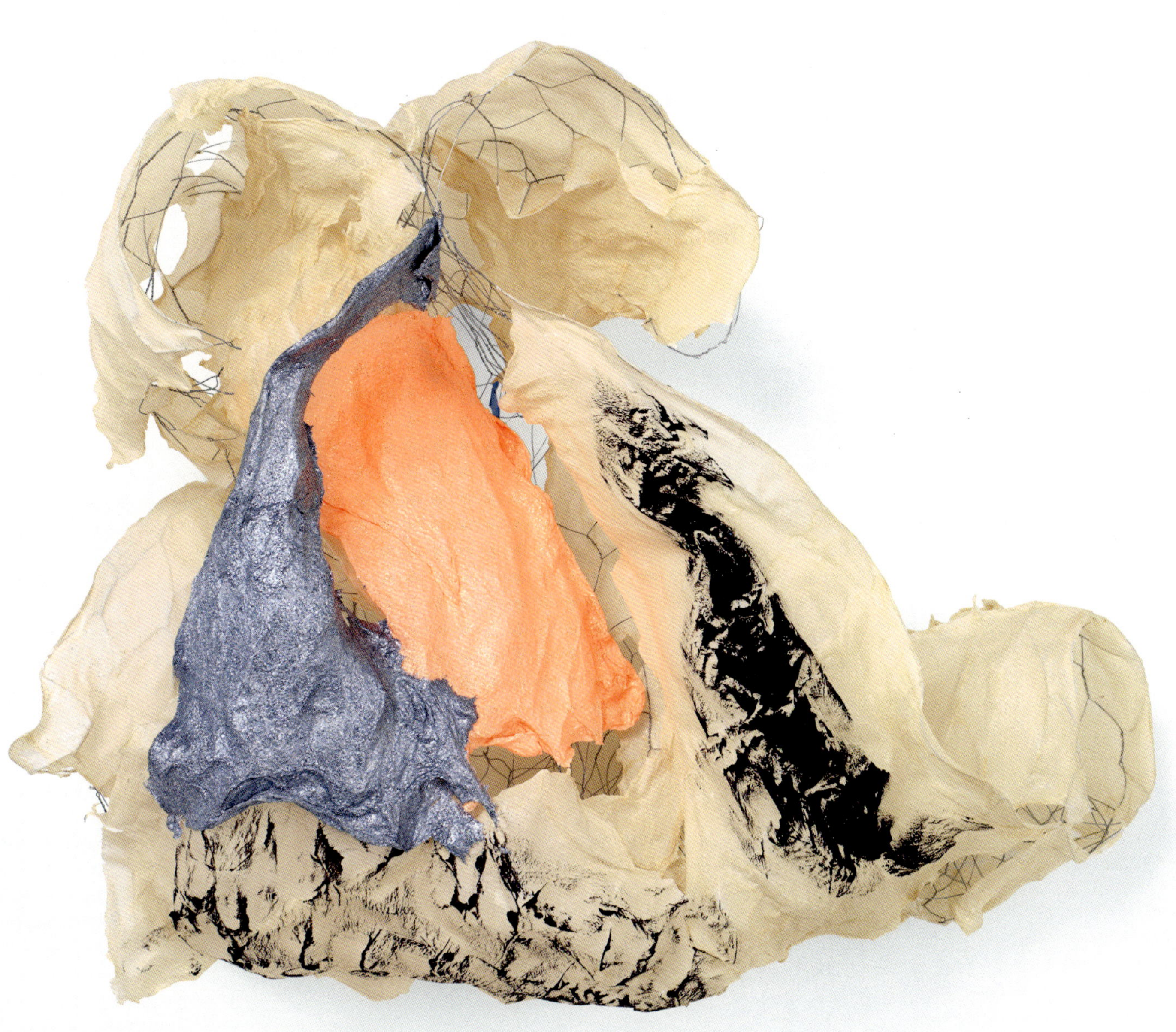

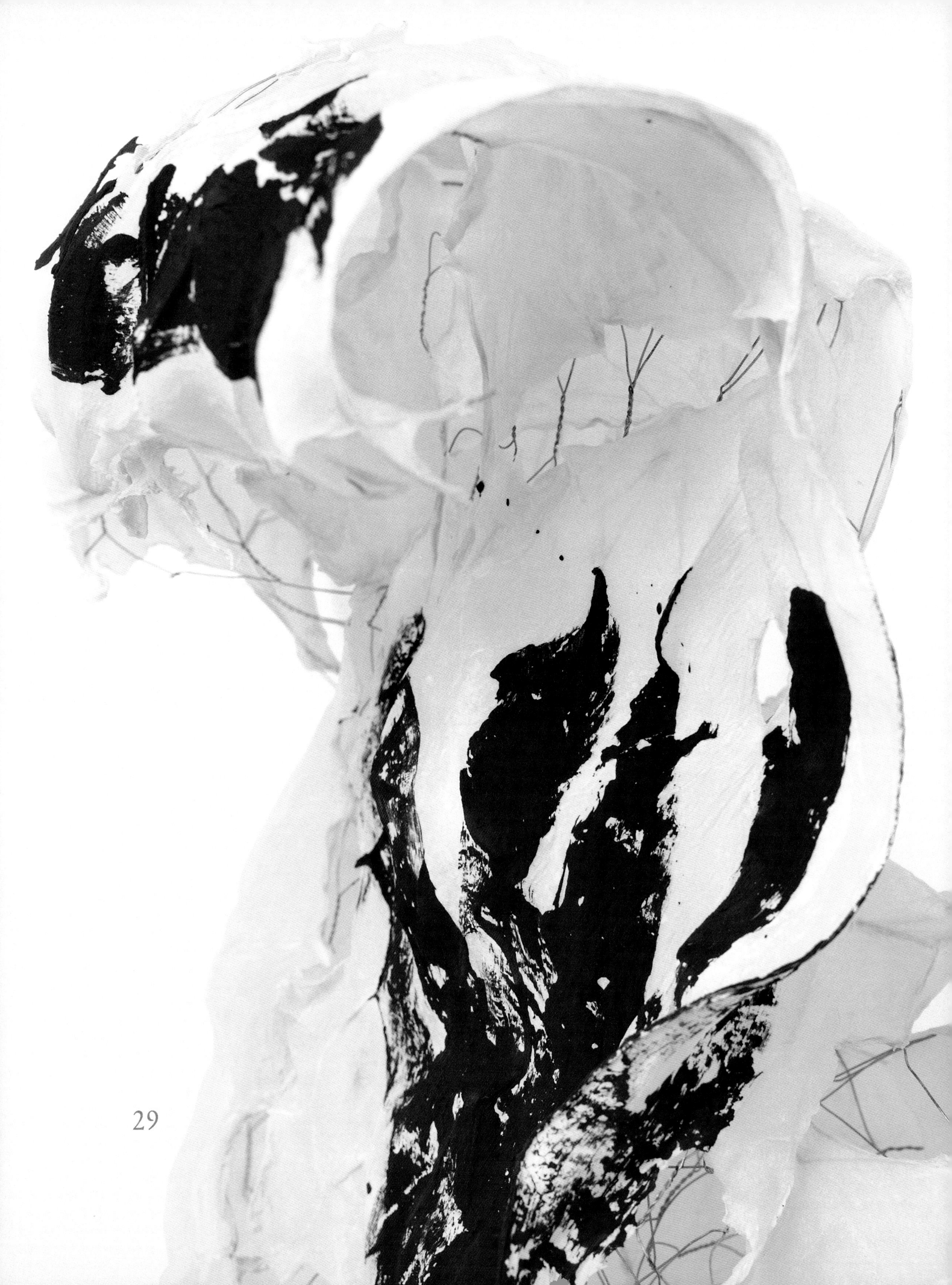

29

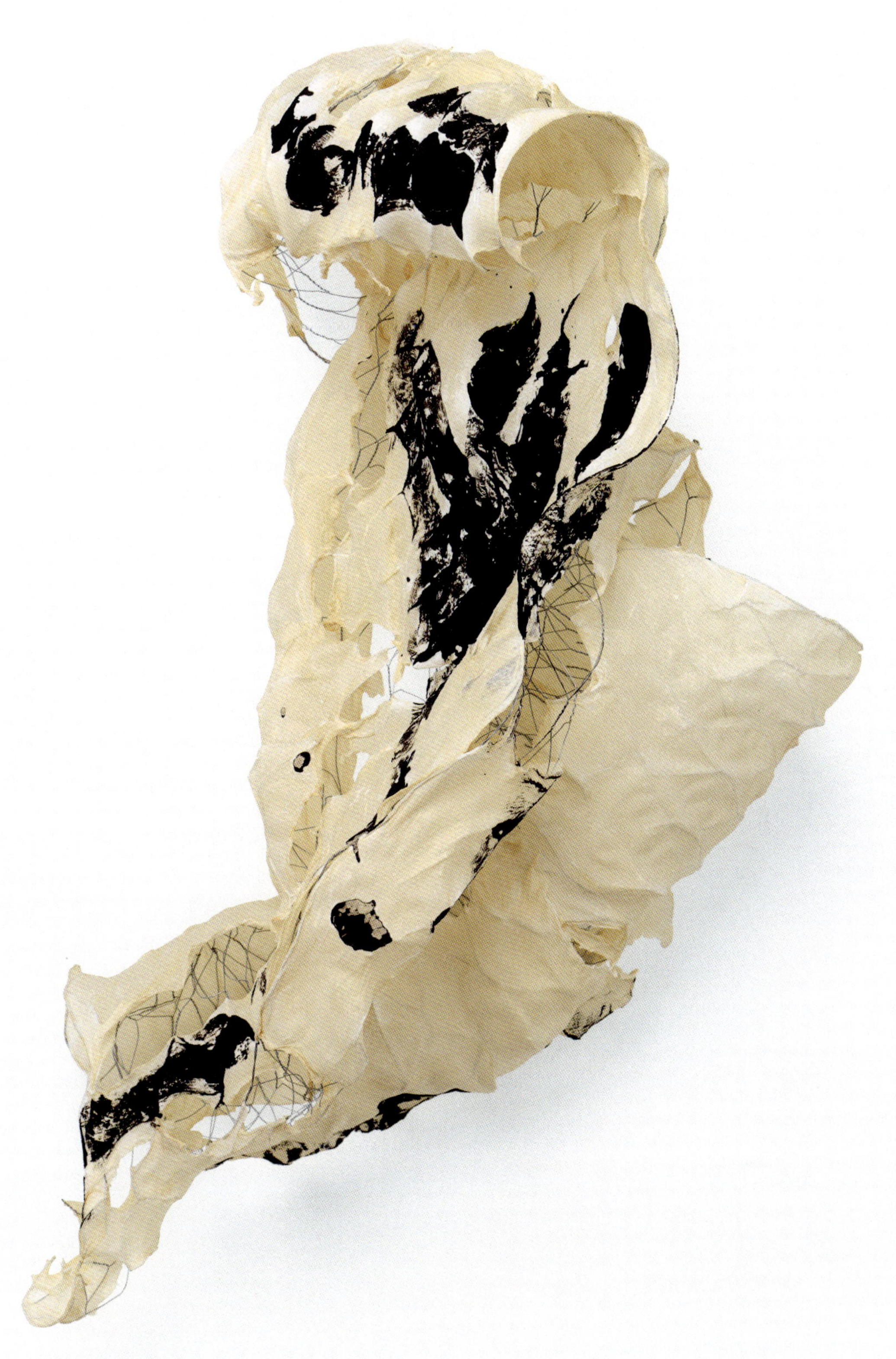

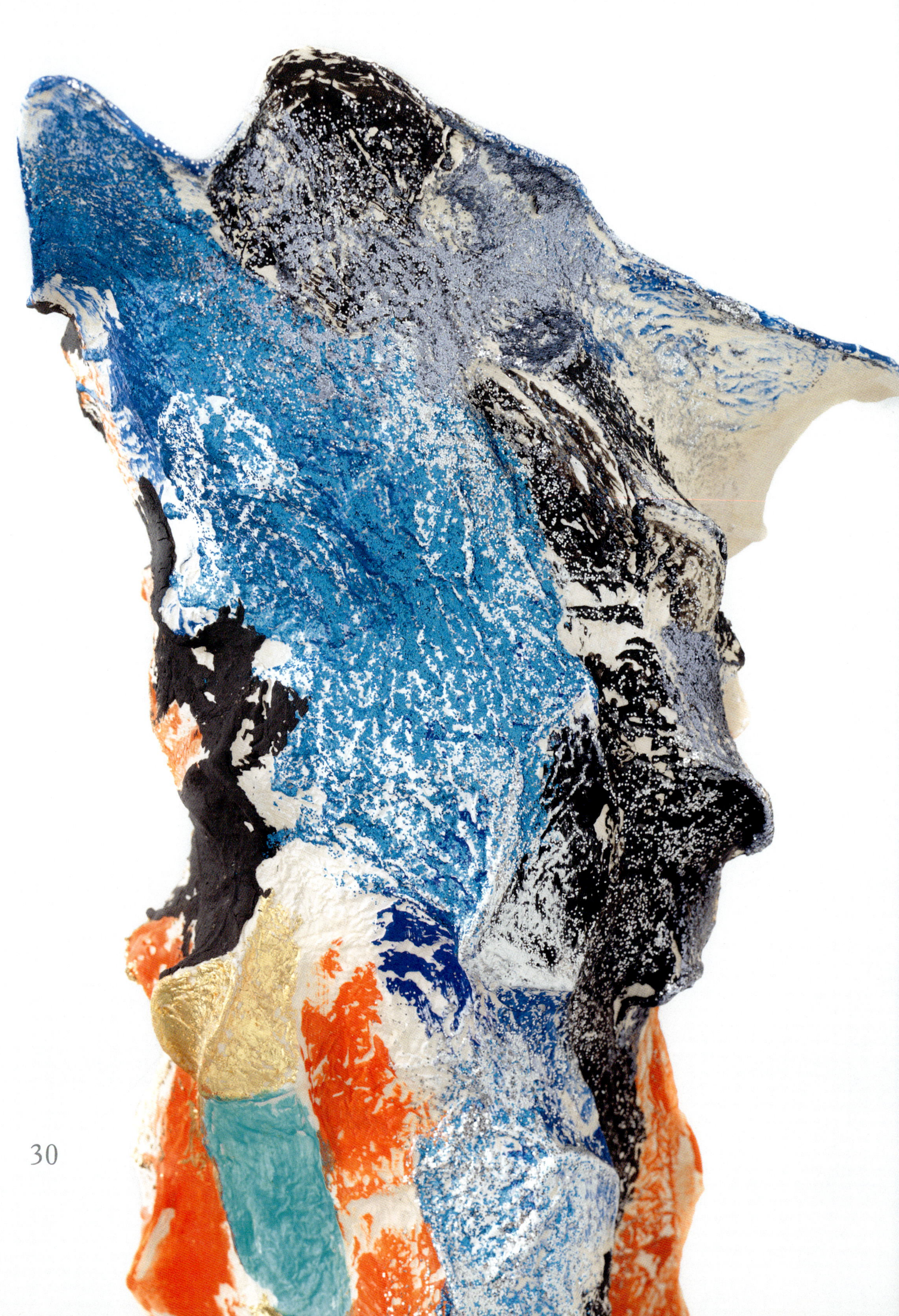

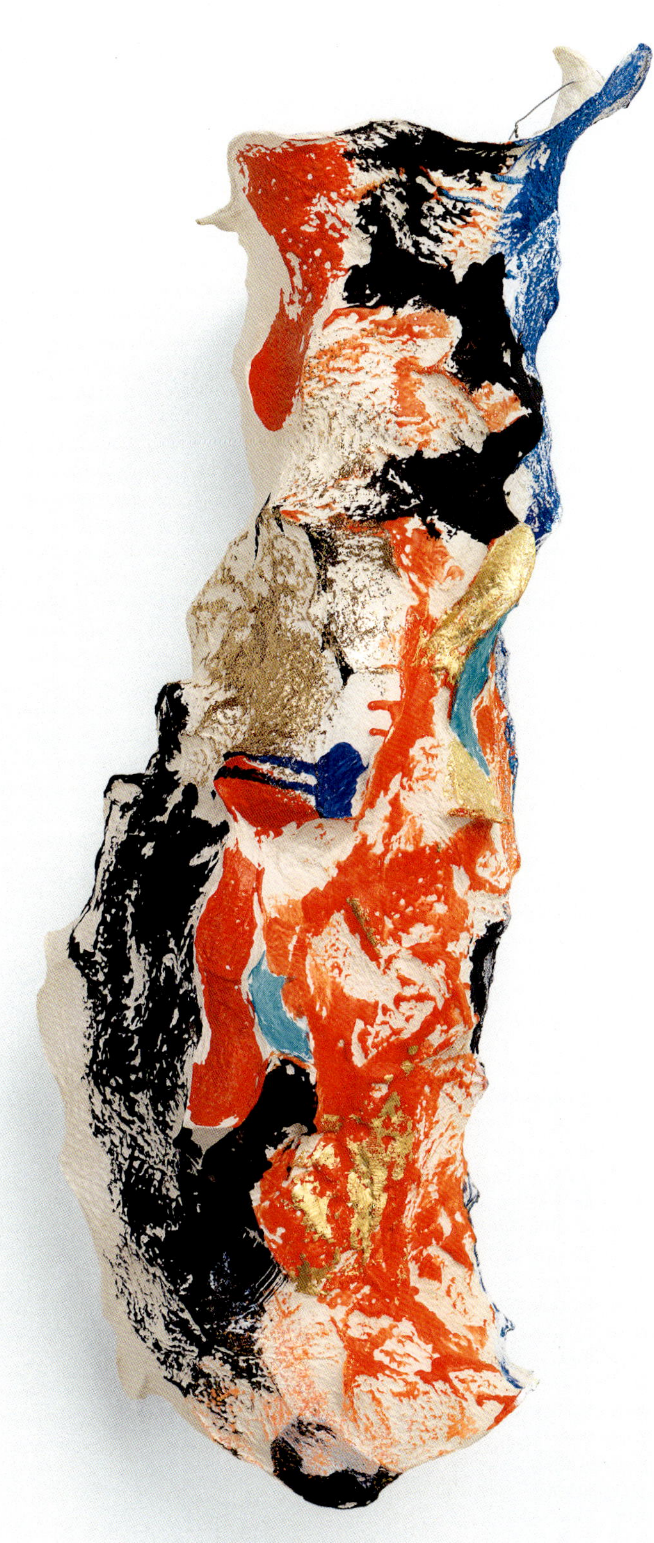

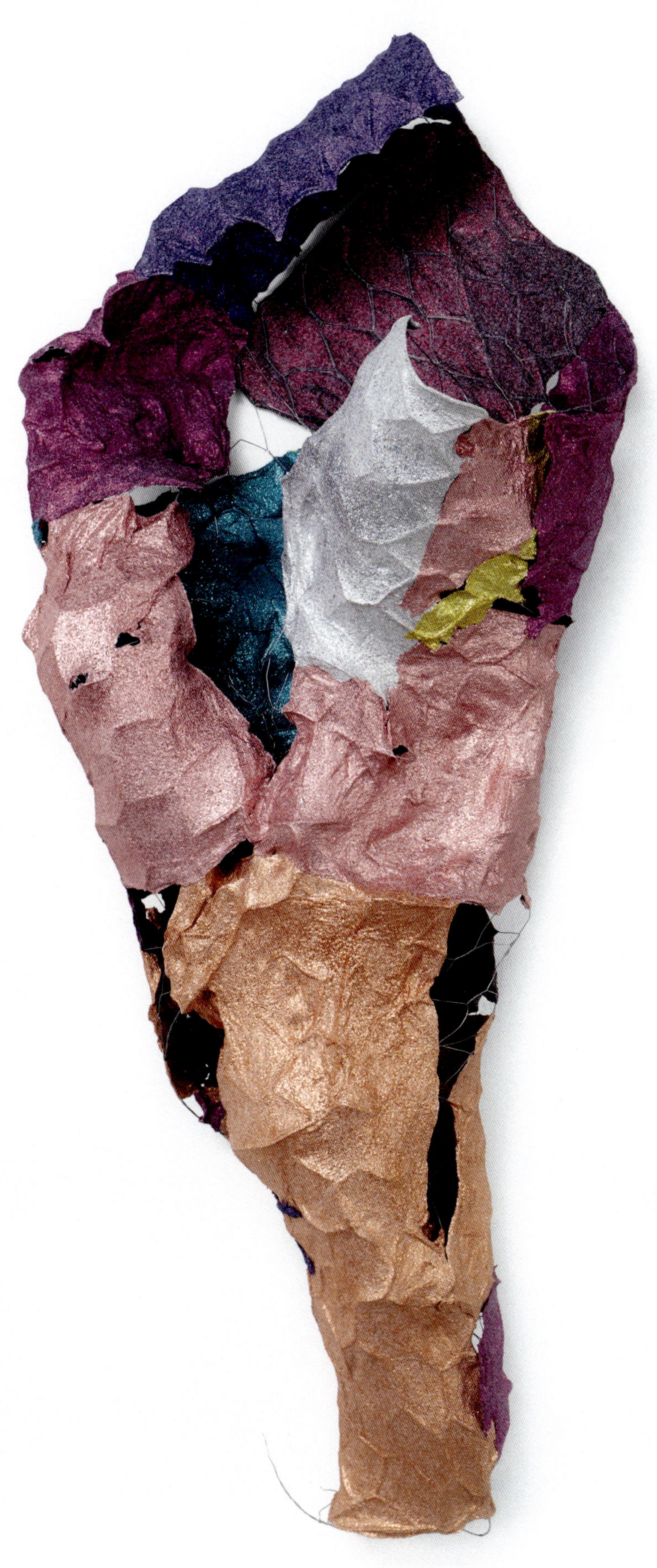

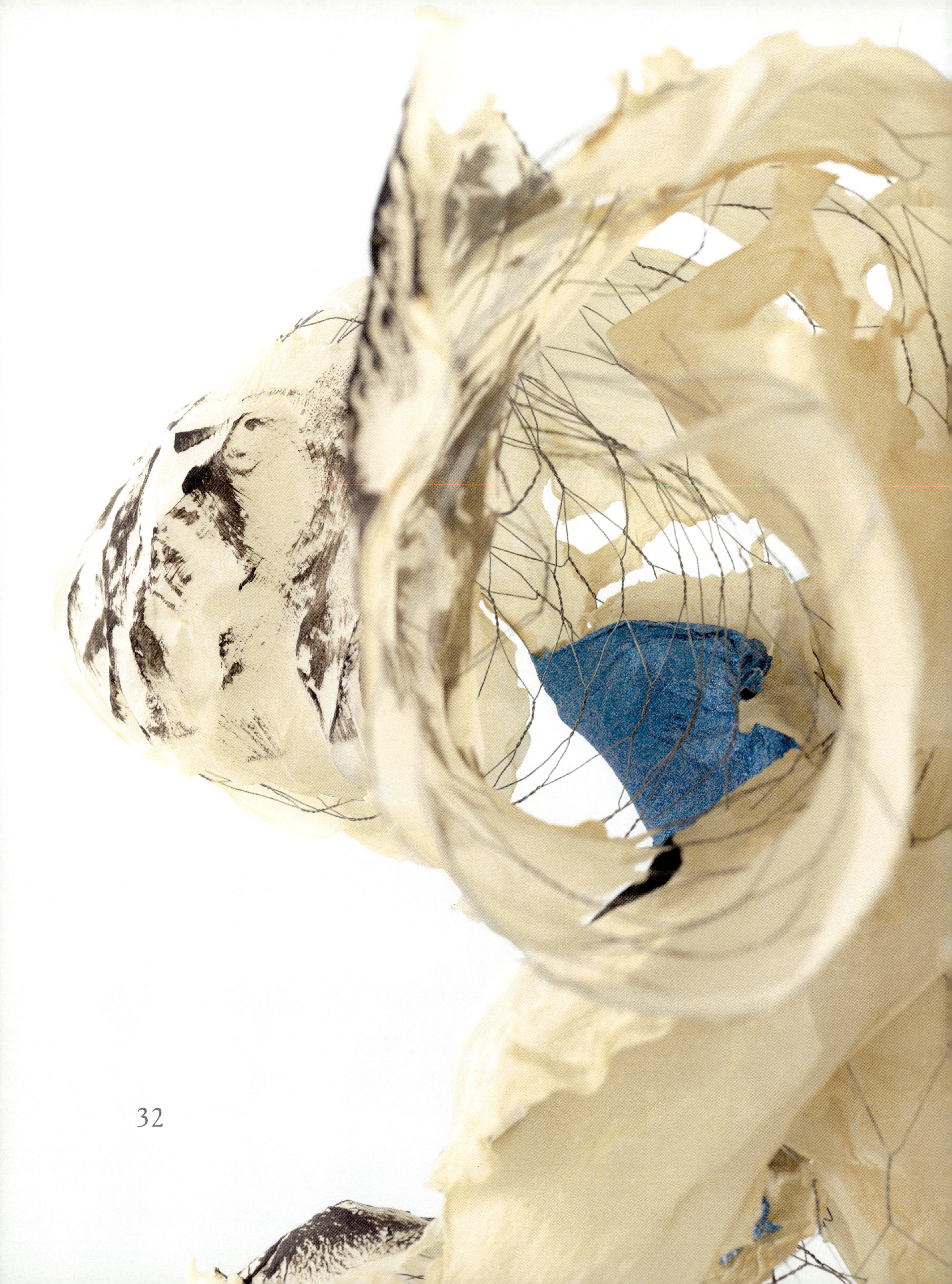

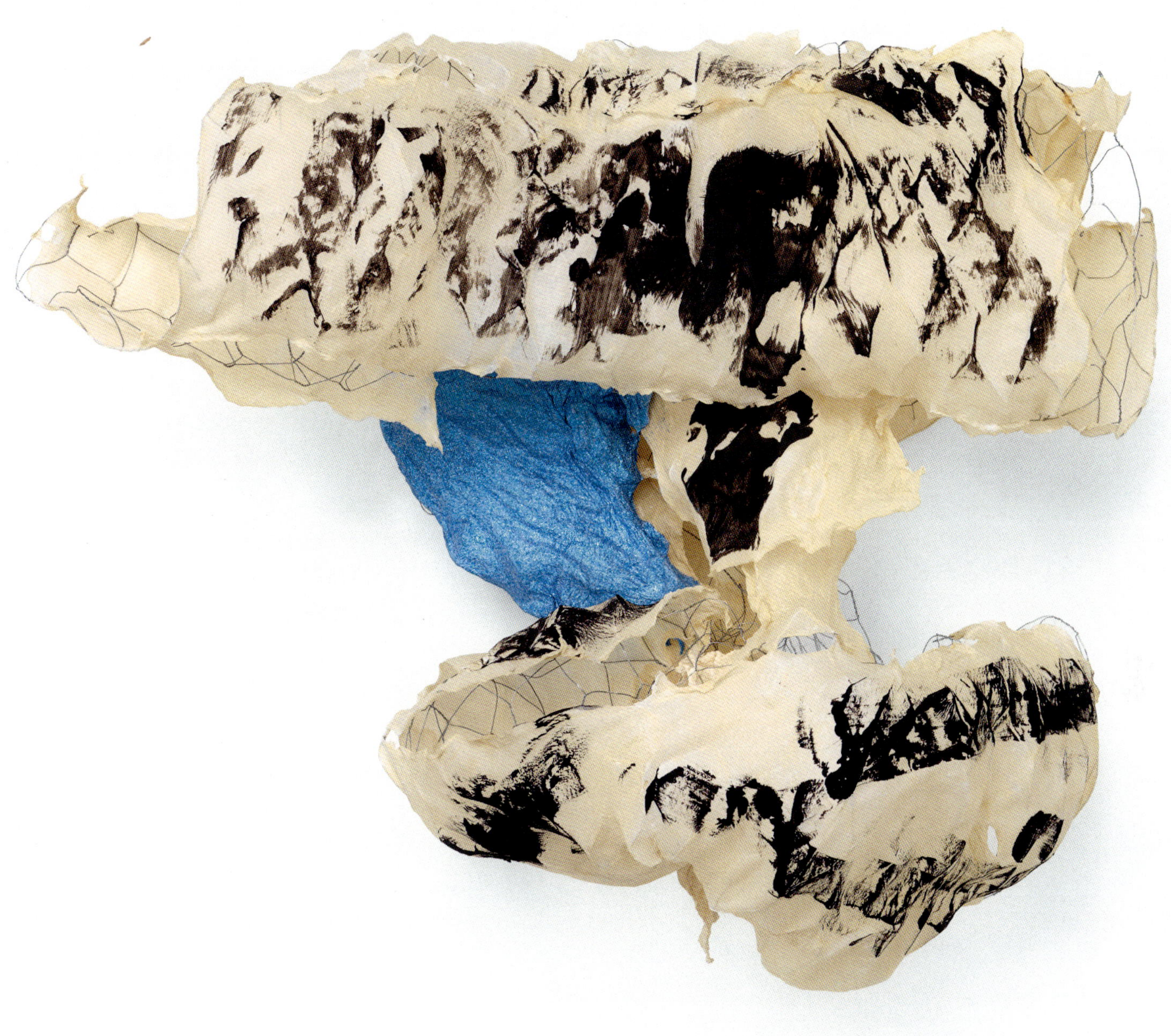

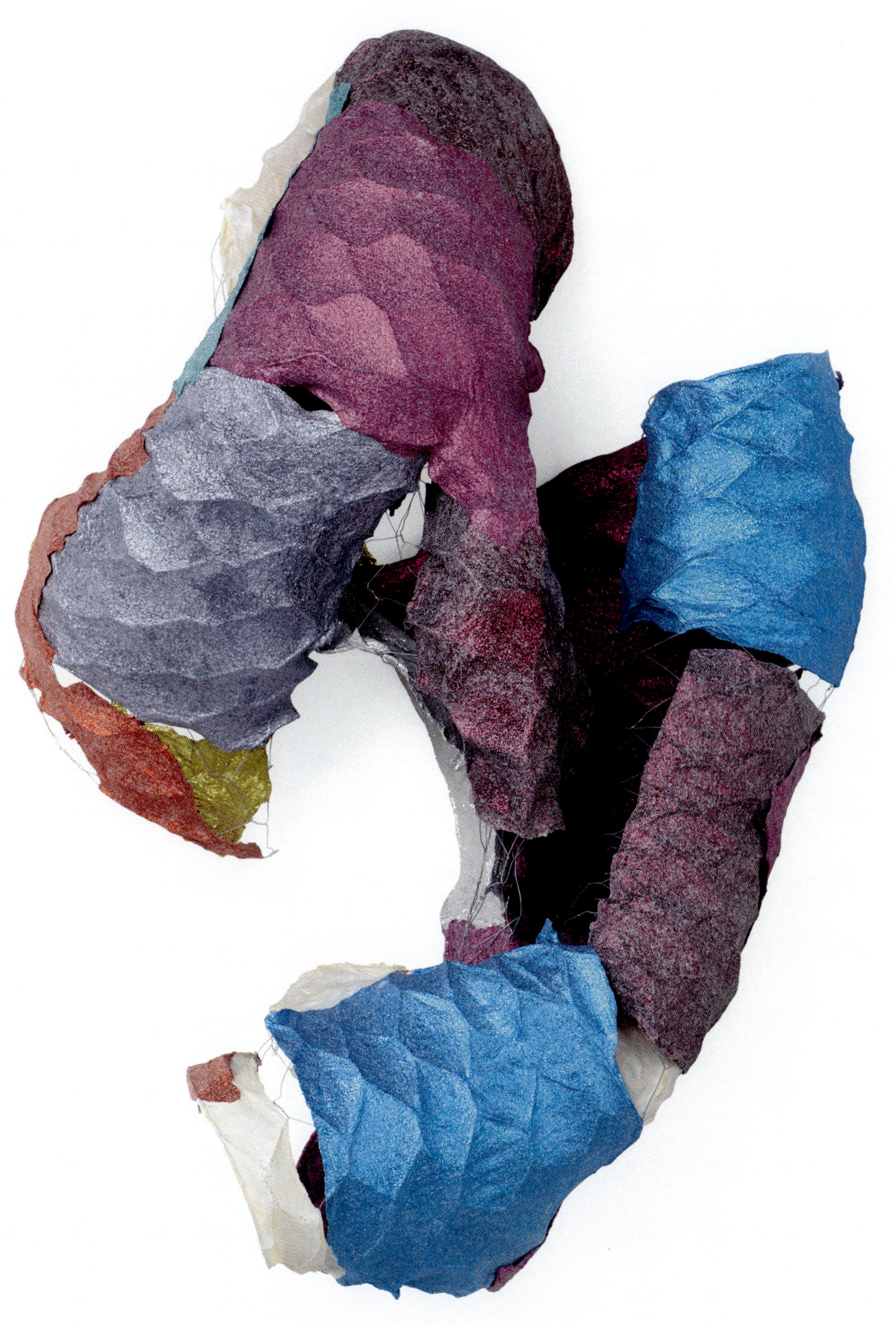

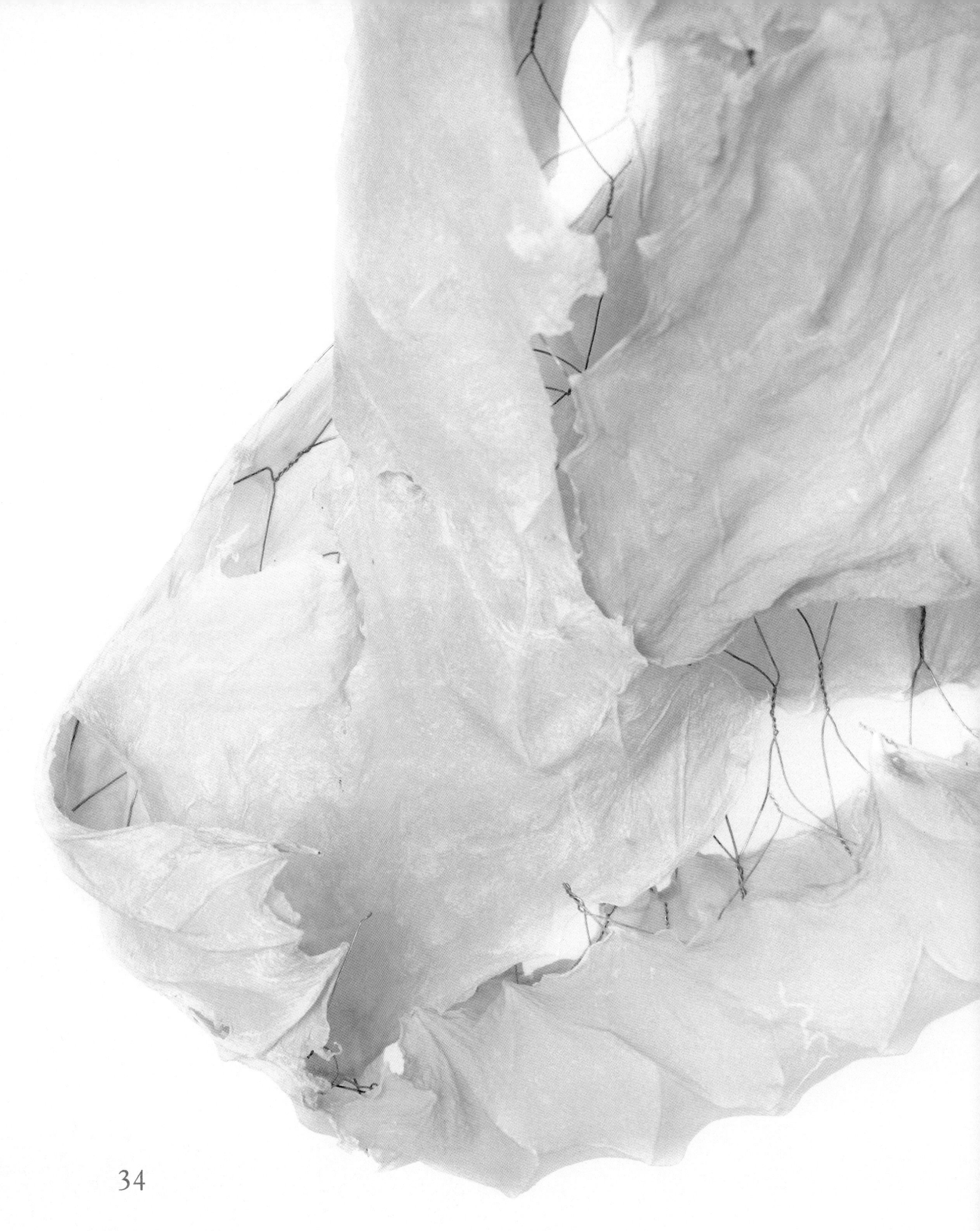

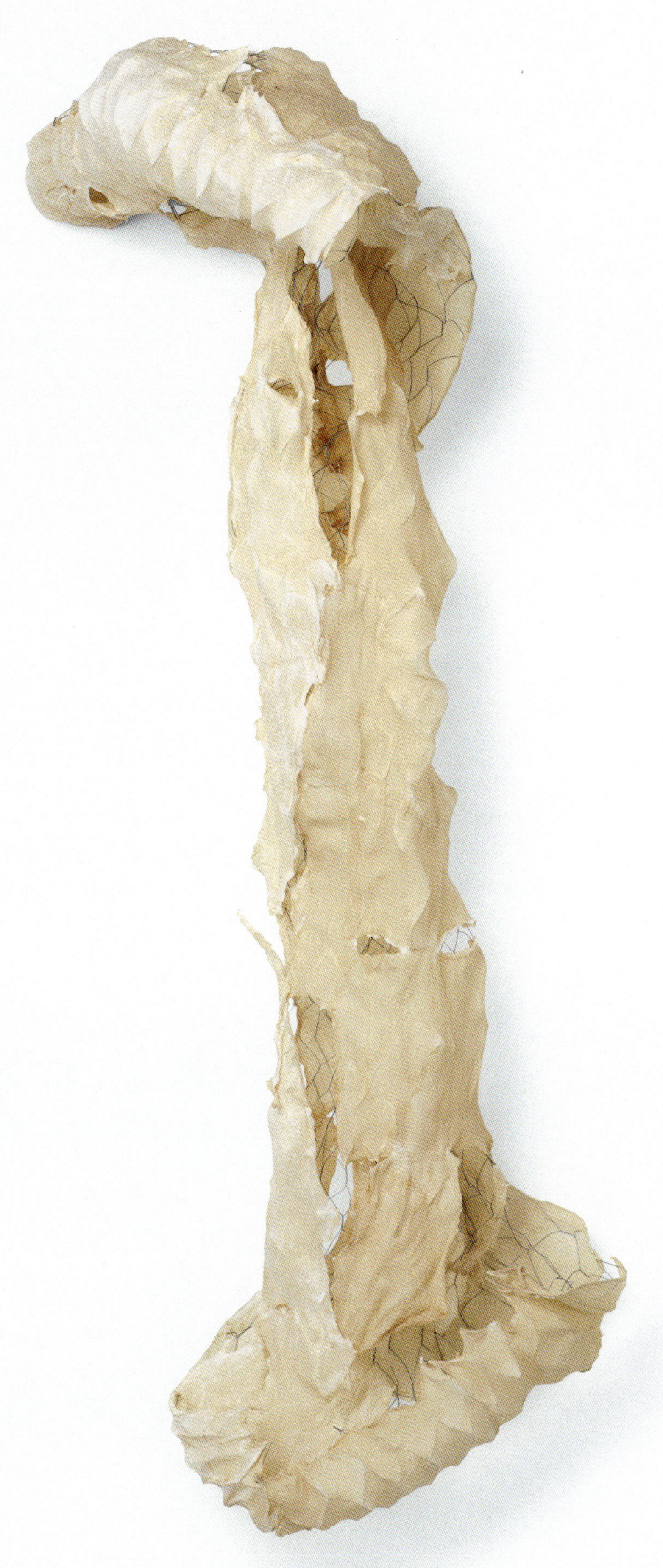

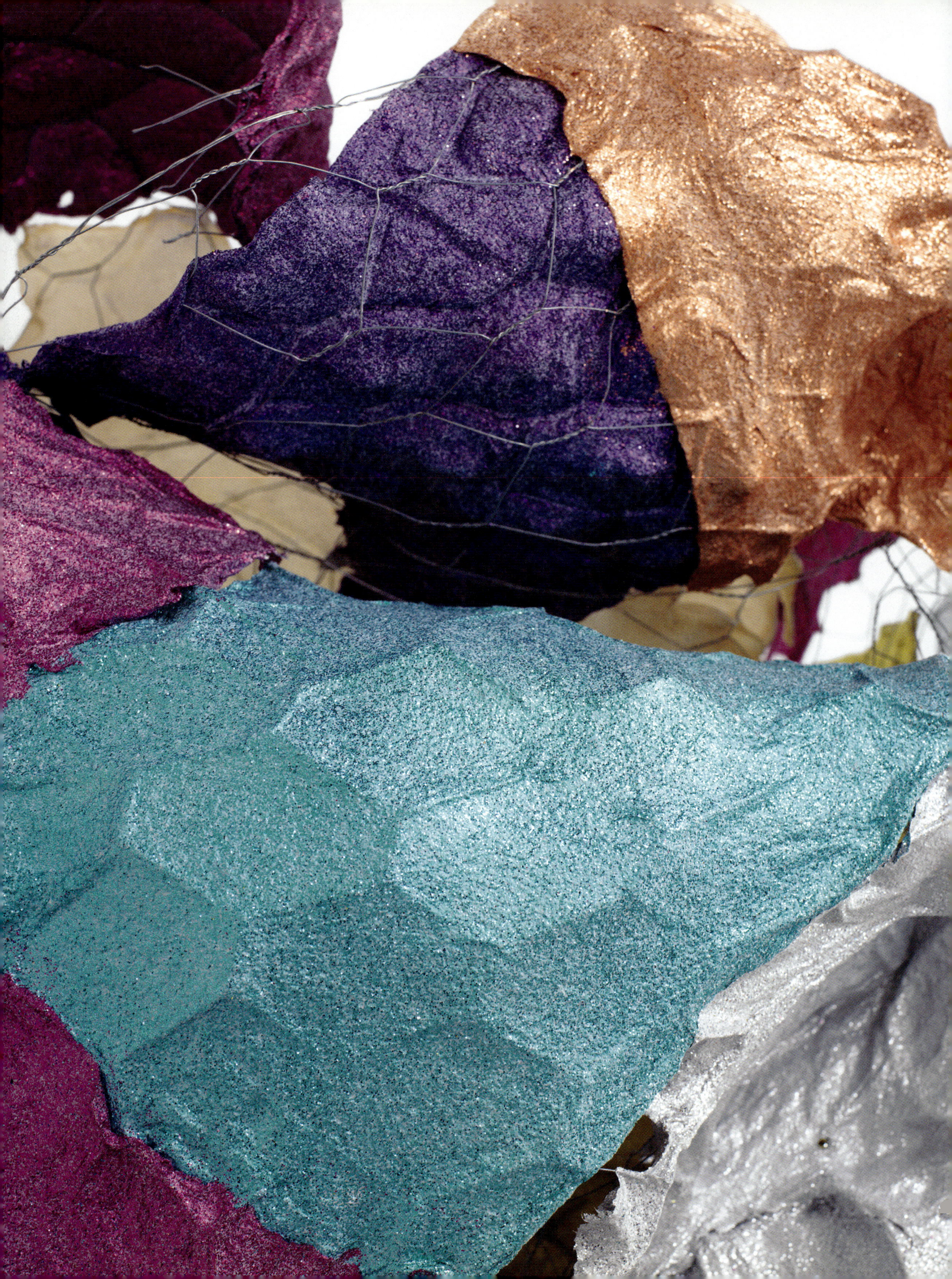

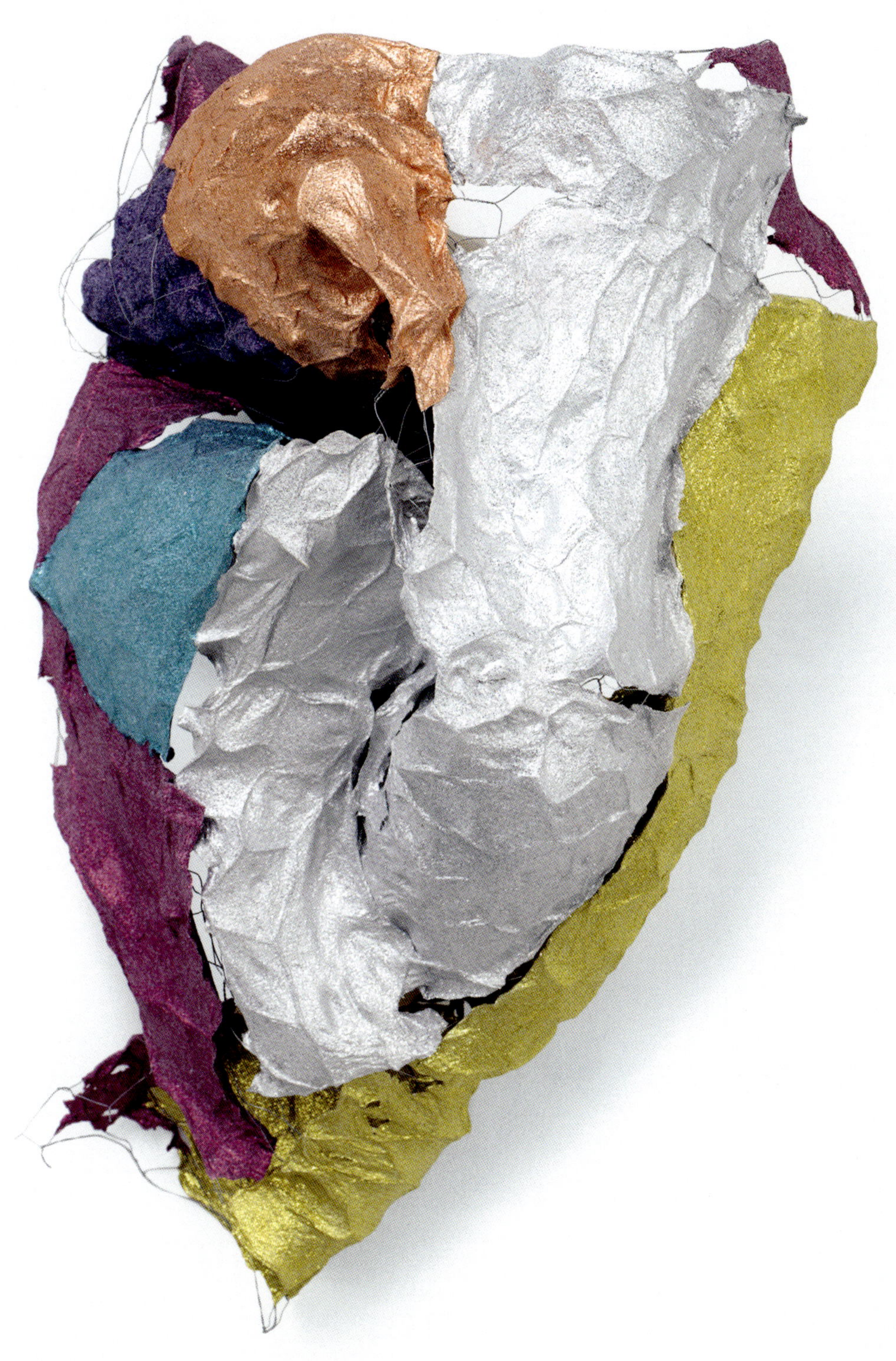

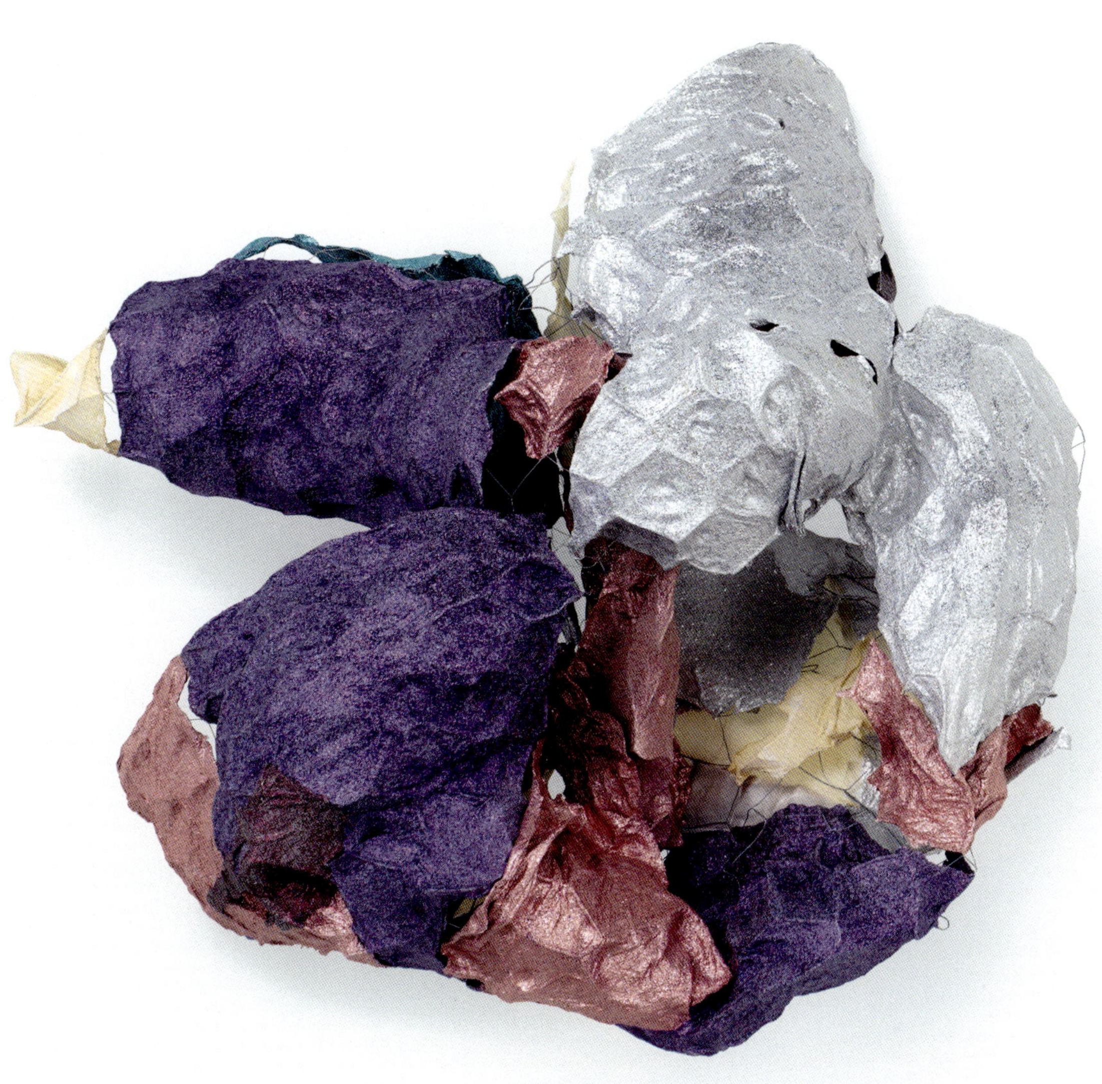

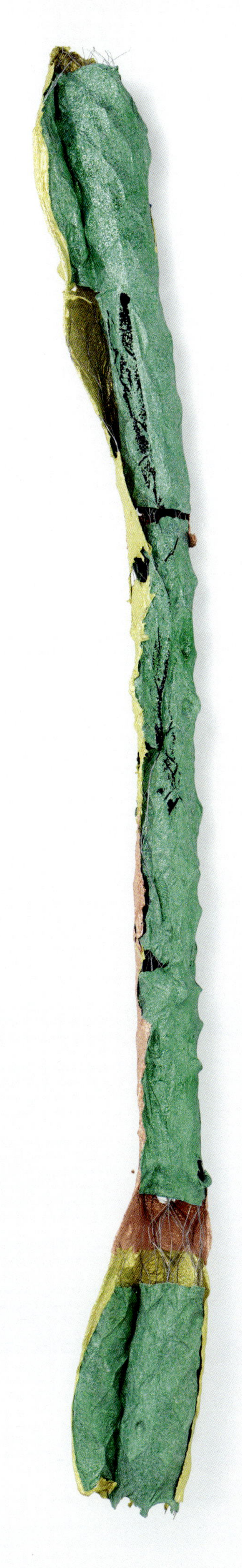

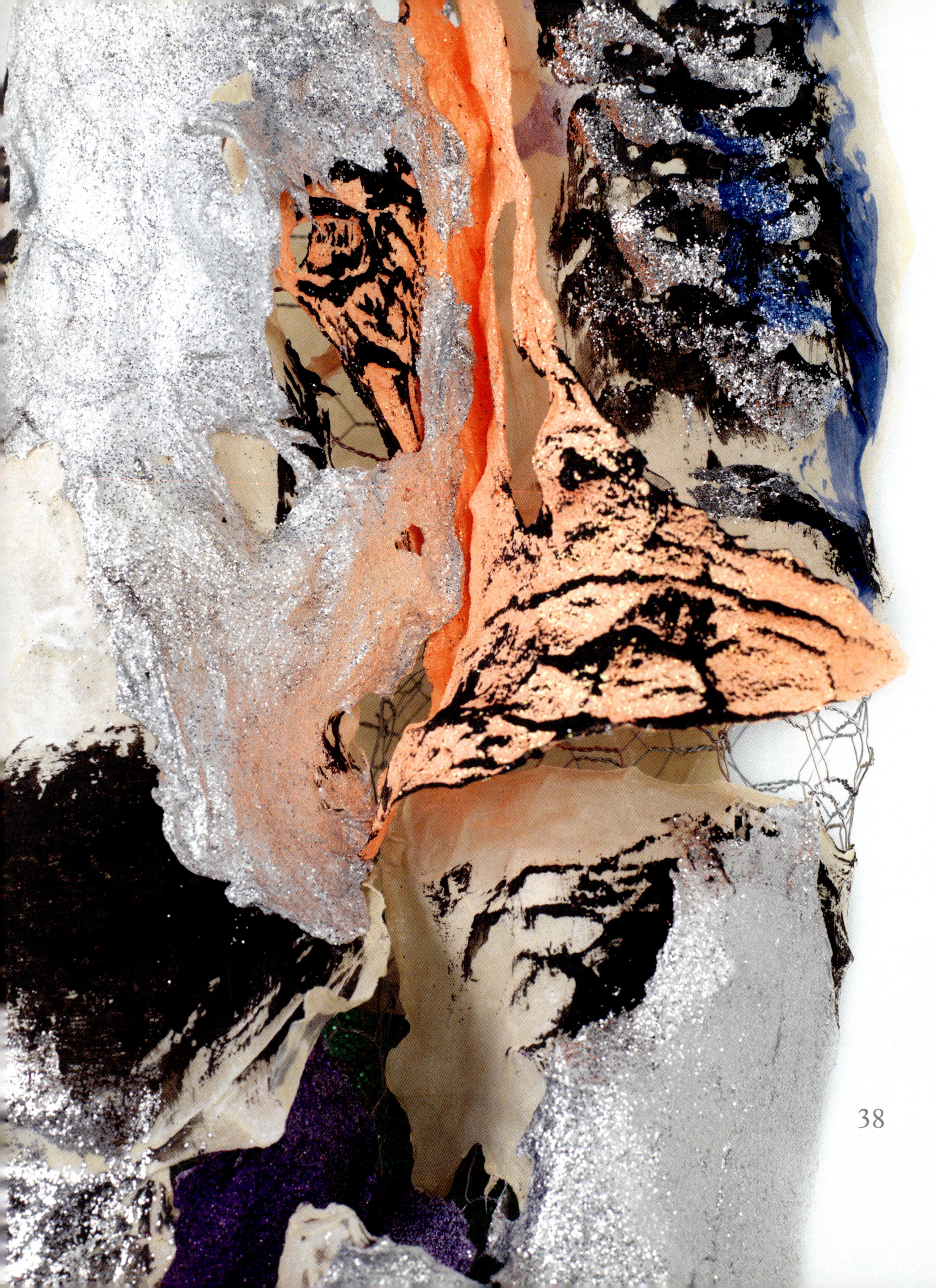

38

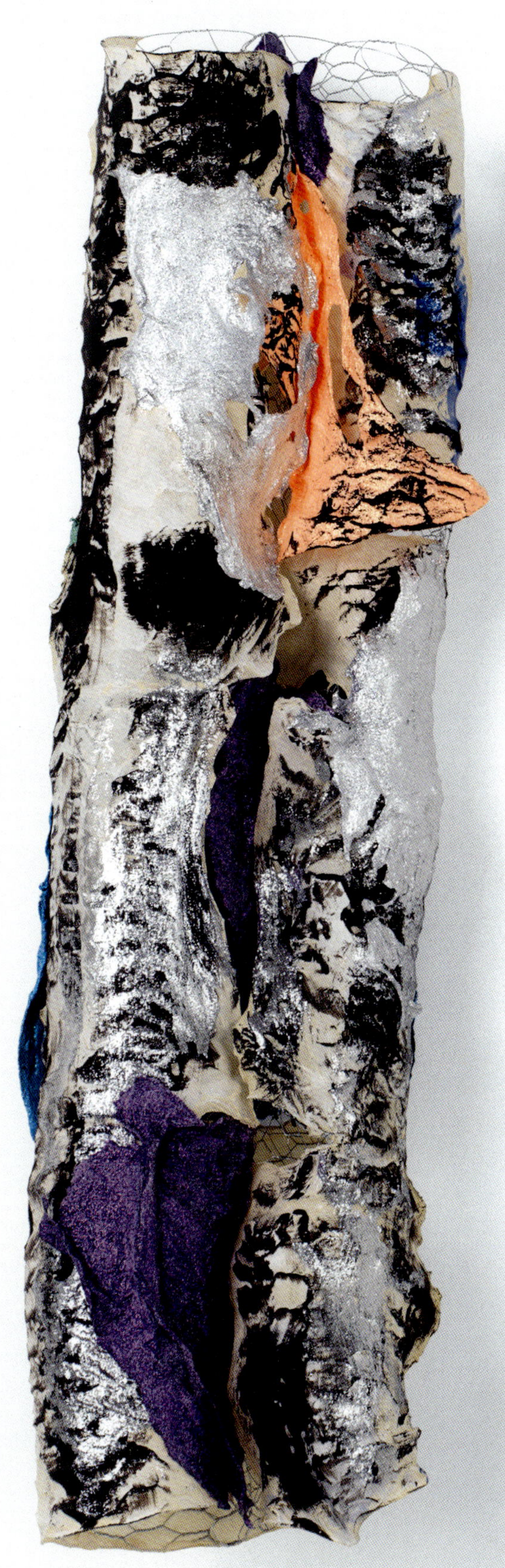

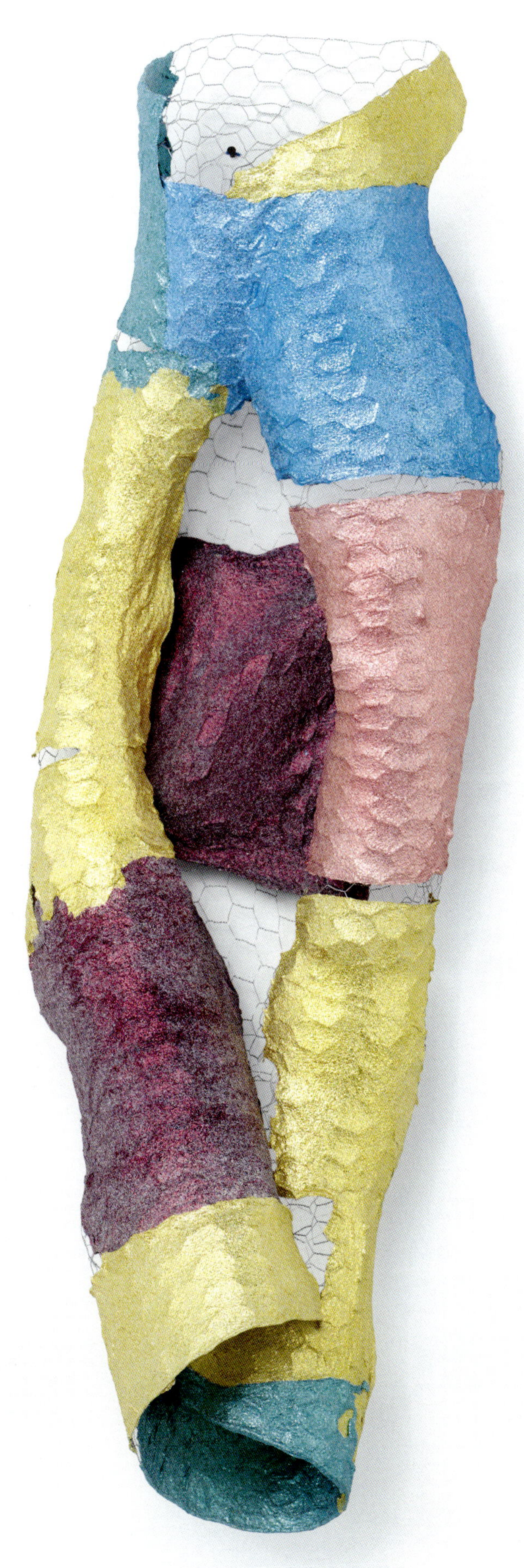

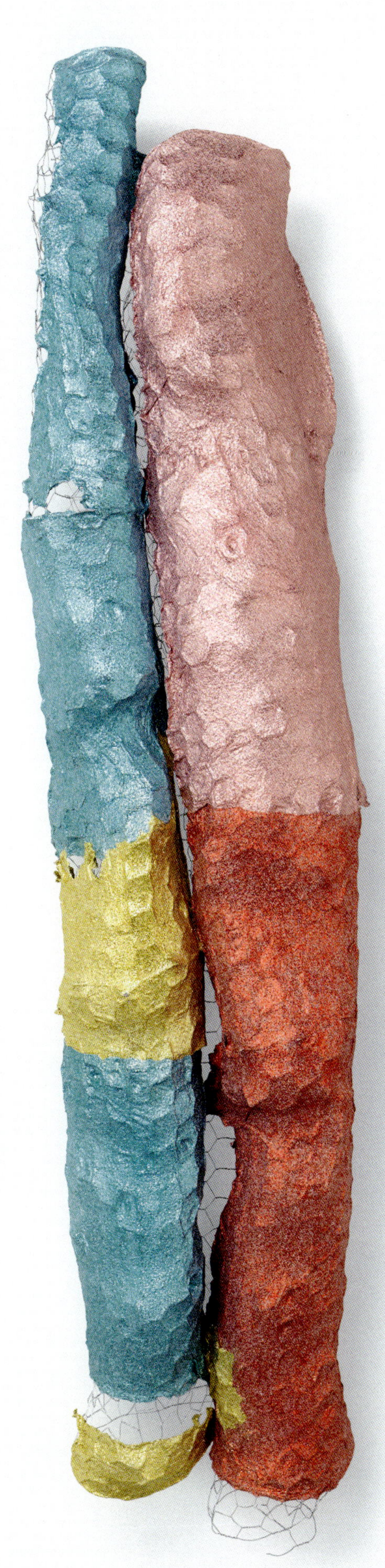

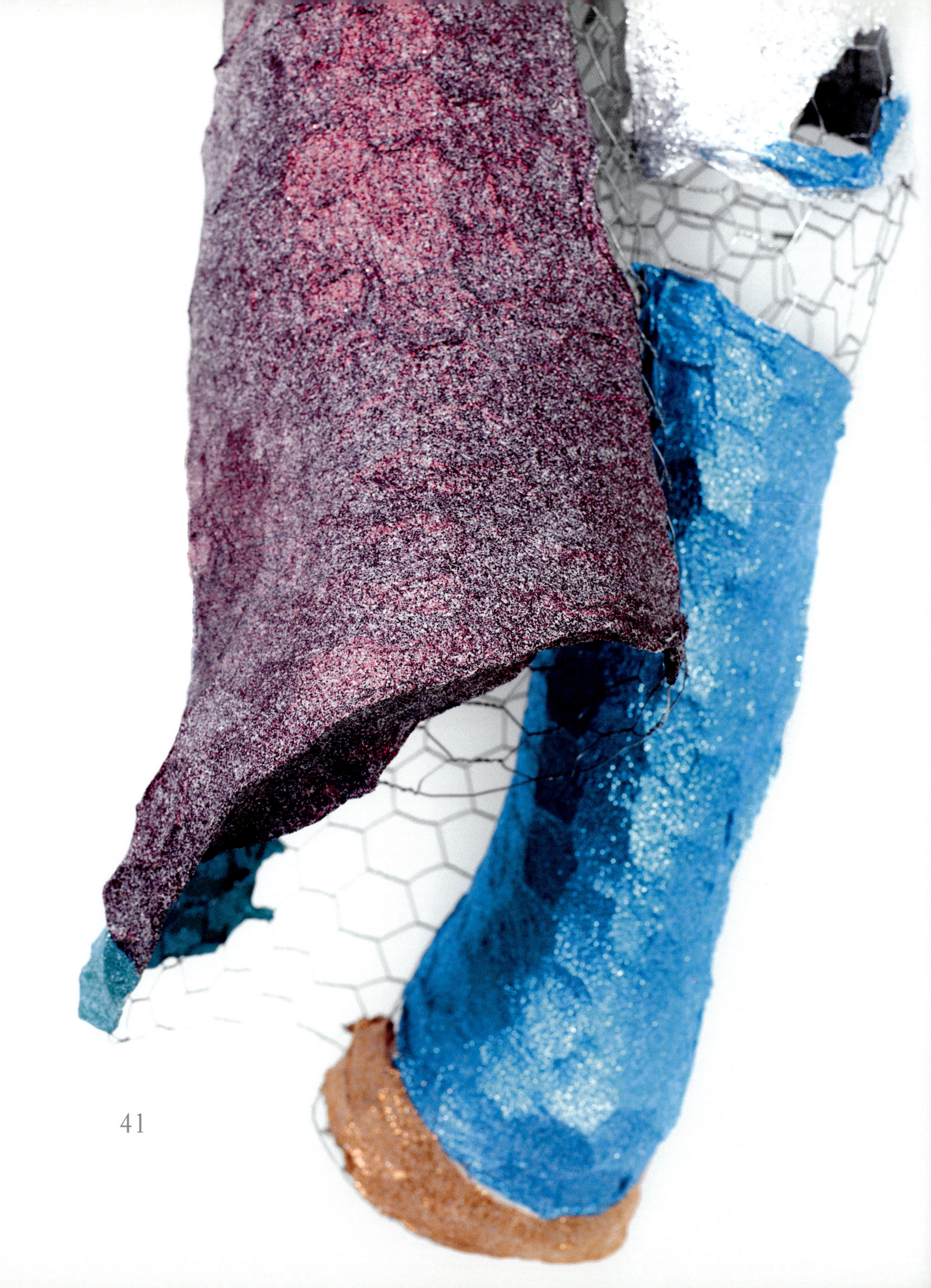

41

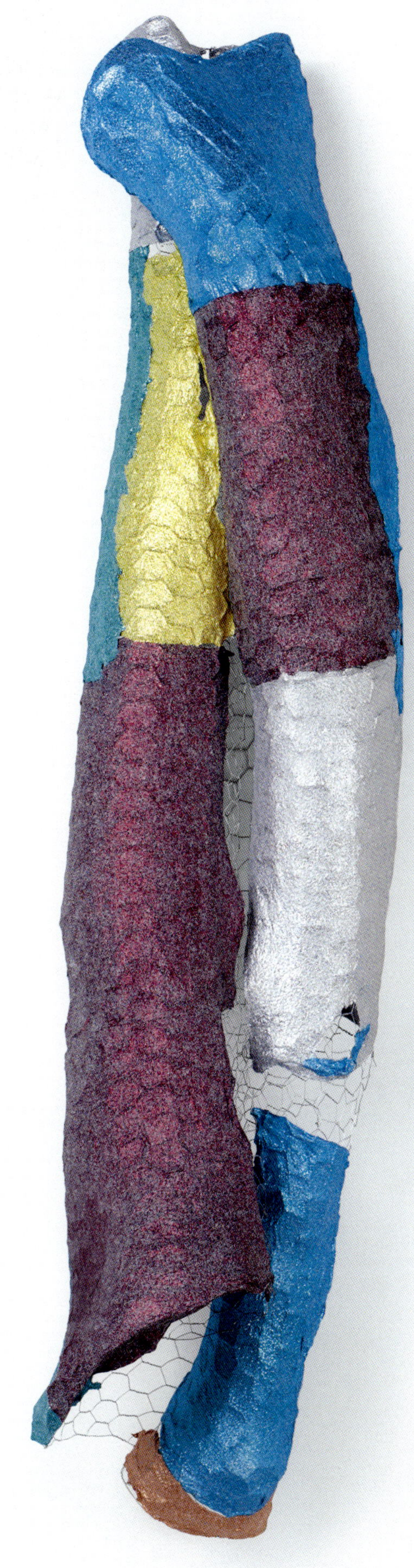

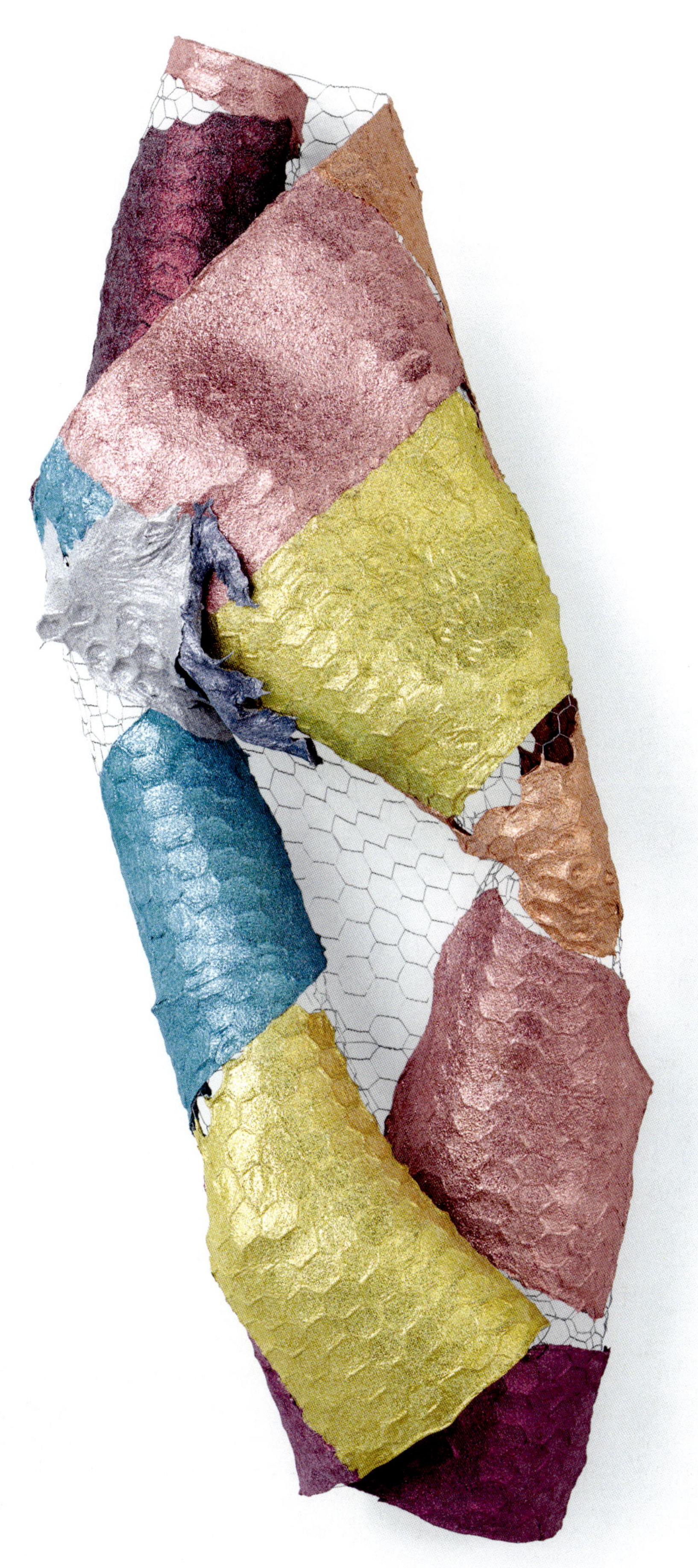

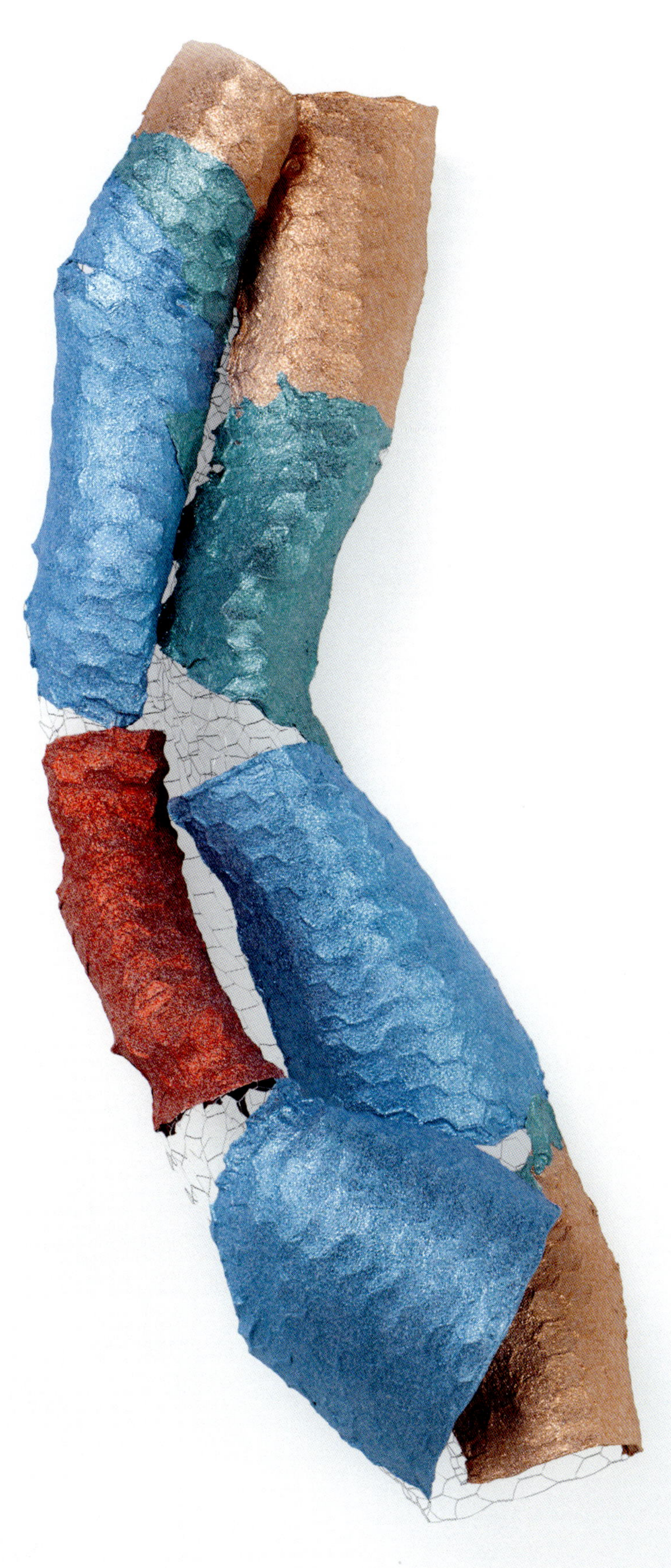

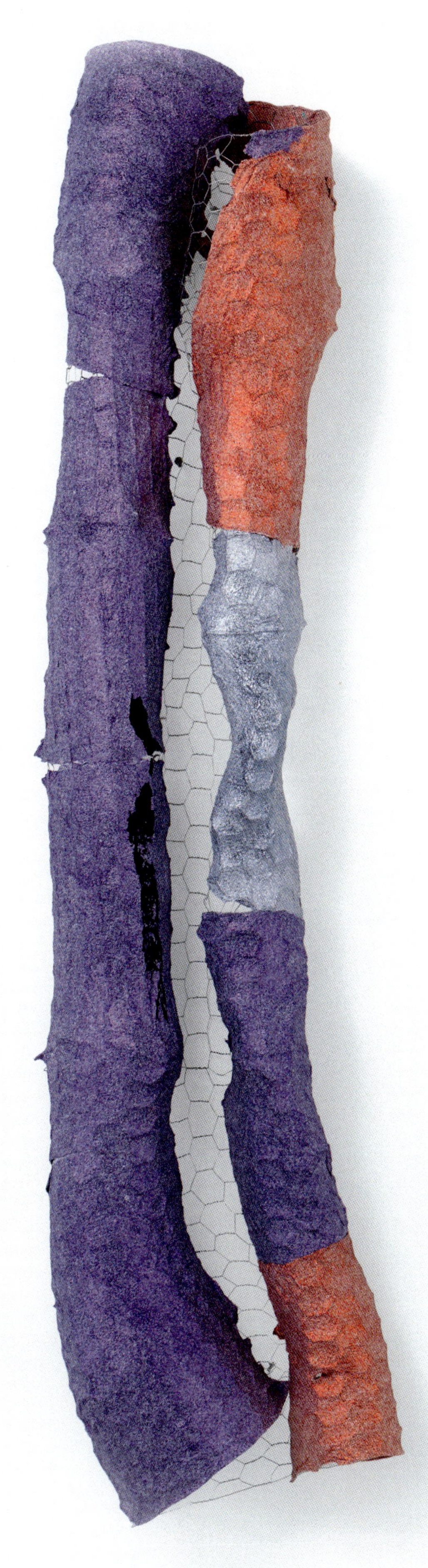

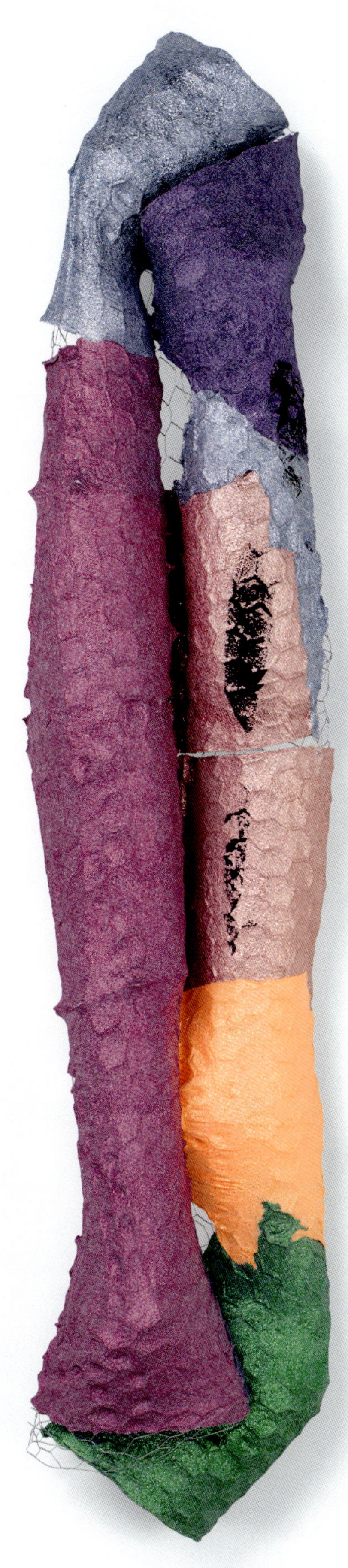

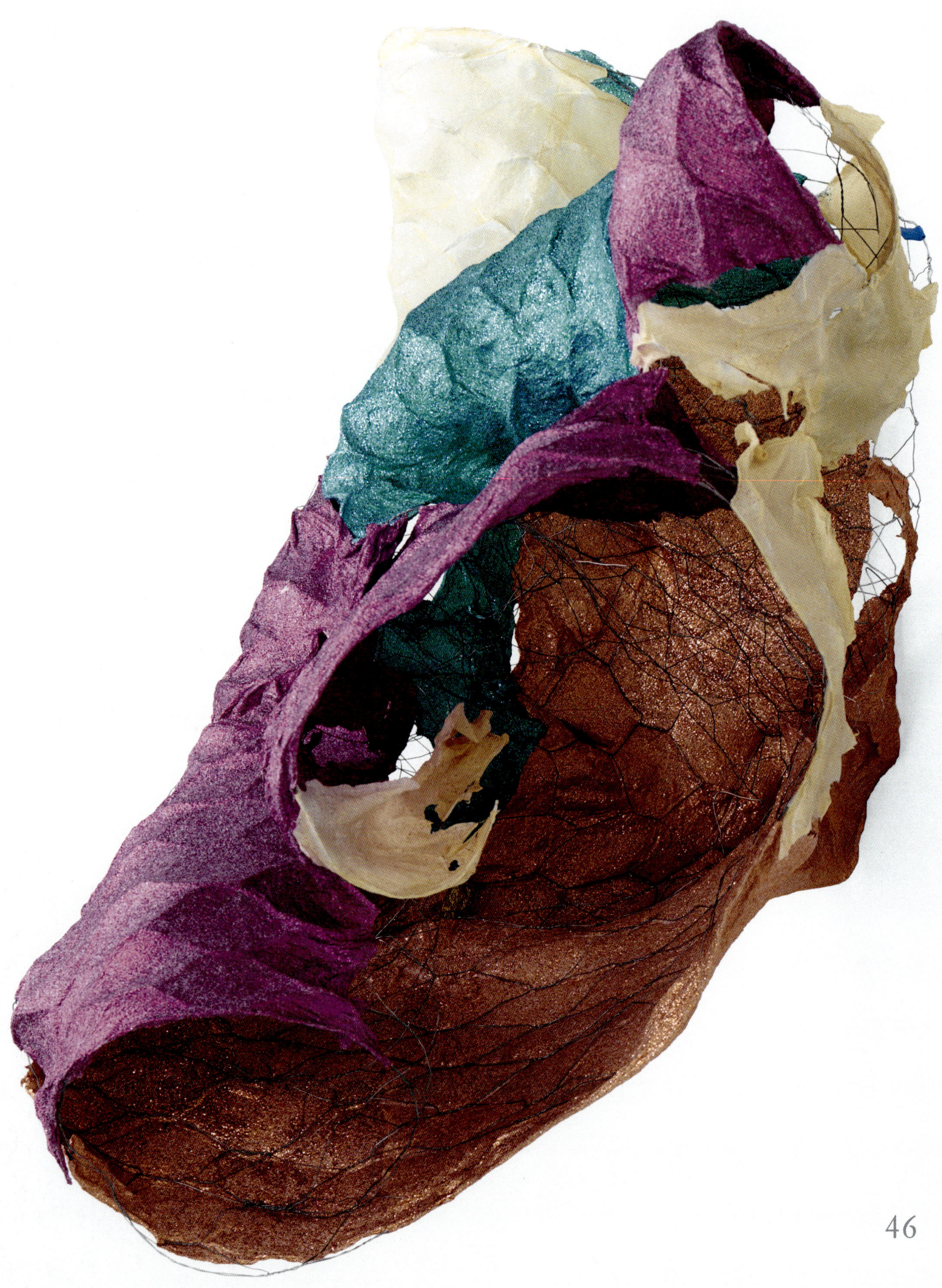

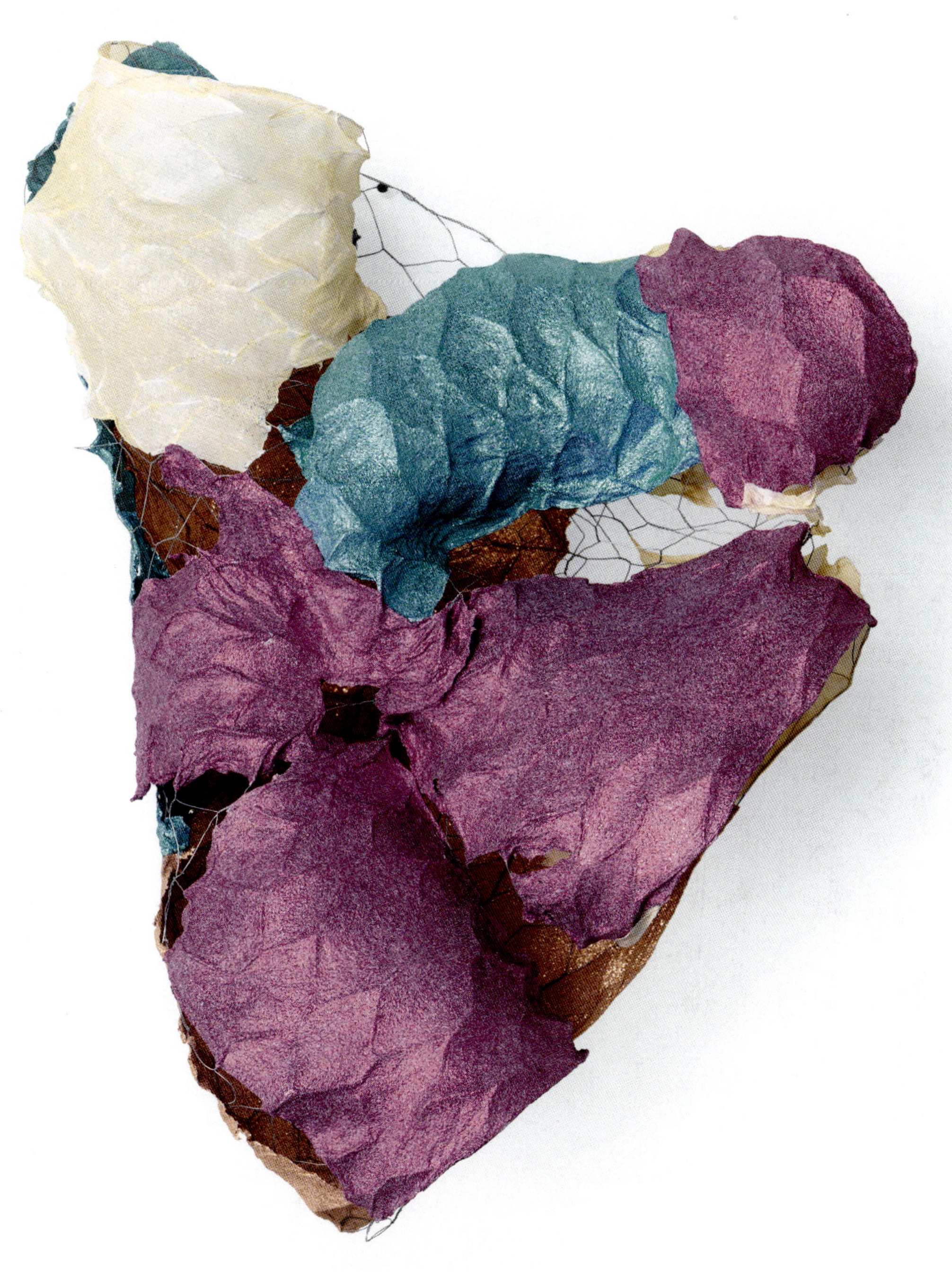

LIST OF PLATES

1. *Saddle Lane (Bull Path Series)* 2013–14
handmade paper over chicken wire, pigmented acrylic medium,
ground coal with matte medium, watercolor, gold leaf
28 1/2 x 11 x 9 in 72.4 x 27.9 x 22.9 cm

2. *Swamp Road (Bull Path Series)* 2013–14
handmade paper over chicken wire, pigmented acrylic medium,
ground coal with matte medium, watercolor, gold leaf
35 1/2 x 14 x 10 in 90.2 x 35.6 x 25.4 cm

3. *European Golden Plover* 2014
handmade paper over chicken wire, encaustic wax, encaustic
wax with India ink
65 x 13 x 13 1/2 in 165.1 x 33 x 34.3 cm

4. *Something Else* 2015
handmade paper over chicken wire, ground coal with matte
medium
55 x 41 x 23 in 139.7 x 104.1 x 58.4 cm

5. *Silver Pair* 2015
handmade paper over chicken wire, acrylic medium, glitter
72 x 10 x 13 1/2 in each 182.9 x 25.4 x 34.3 cm each

6. *Silver "Zip" (For Barney)* 2015
handmade paper over chicken wire, ground coal with matte
medium, acrylic, acrylic medium, silver leaf glitter
68 x 14 x 18 1/2 in 172.7 x 35.6 x 47 cm

7. *Broken Favor II* 2015–16
handmade paper over chicken wire, ground coal with matte
medium, acrylic, acrylic medium, glitter
25 x 21 x 15 in 63.5 x 53.3 x 38.1 cm

8. *Bee Sting* 2015
handmade paper over chicken wire
64 x 21 x 24 in 162.6 x 53.3 x 61 cm

9. *Broken Favor I* 2015–16
handmade paper over chicken wire, ground coal with matte
medium, acrylic, acrylic medium, glitter
36 x 21 x 10 in 91.4 x 53.3 x 25.4 cm

10. *Look Back* 2015–16
handmade paper over chicken wire, cast glitter on handmade
paper, ground coal with matte medium
71 x 16 1/2 x 19 in 180.3 x 41.9 x 48.3 cm

11. *Triple Spot* 2015–16
handmade paper over chicken wire, ground coal with matte medium
83 x 19 x 19 in 210.8 x 48.3 x 48.3 cm

12. *Sparkle Flag Fern* 2016
handmade paper over chicken wire, cast glitter on handmade paper
78 x 19 x 23 in 198.1 x 48.3 x 58.4 cm

13. *Butterfly Tube* 2015
handmade paper over chicken wire
26 x 22 x 12 1/2 in 66 x 55.9 x 31.8 cm

14. *Little Silver Spirit* 2015–16
handmade paper over chicken wire, cast glitter on handmade
paper, ground coal with matte medium, acrylic, acrylic
medium, glitter
33 x 10 1/2 x 8 in 83.8 x 26.7 x 20.3 cm

15. *Curtains* 2015–16
handmade paper over chicken wire, acrylic, acrylic medium,
glitter
66 x 22 x 18 in 167.6 x 55.9 x 45.7 cm

16. *Fan Farinade* 2016
handmade paper over chicken wire
58 x 31 x 19 in 147.3 x 78.7 x 48.3 cm

17. *Swift* 2015
handmade paper over chicken wire, ground coal with matte
medium, acrylic medium, glitter
27 1/2 x 26 x 13 in 69.9 x 66 x 33 cm

18. *Woopee* 2015
handmade paper over chicken wire, ground coal with matte
medium, acrylic medium, glitter
33 x 20 x 14 in 83.8 x 50.8 x 35.6 cm

19. *Vested Spirit* 2015
handmade paper over chicken wire, ground coal with matte
medium, acrylic medium, gold glitter, glitter
36 1/2 x 16 x 11 in 92.7 x 40.6 x 27.9 cm

20. *Misty Drawing* 2015
handmade paper over chicken wire, acrylic medium, glitter
32 x 12 x 13 1/2 in 81.3 x 30.5 x 34.3 cm

21. *Tree Nest* 2015–16
handmade paper over chicken wire, acrylic, acrylic medium,
glitter
83 x 20 x 15 in 210.8 x 50.8 x 38.1 cm

22. *Hinged Fern* 2015–16
handmade paper over chicken wire, cast glitter on handmade
paper, ground coal with matte medium, acrylic medium, glitter
89 x 28 x 14 1/2 in 226.1 x 71.1 x 36.8 cm

23. *Tree Fern* 2015
handmade paper over chicken wire, acrylic medium, glitter
69 x 21 x 17 in 175.3 x 53.3 x 43.2 cm

24. *Goat's Fern* 2015–16
handmade paper over chicken wire, ground coal with matte
medium, acrylic, acrylic medium, glitter
73 x 23 x 19 in 185.4 x 58.4 x 48.3 cm

25. *Attitude* 2015–16
handmade paper over chicken wire, ground coal with matte medium, acrylic, acrylic medium, glitter
57 x 14 x 11 in 144.8 x 35.6 x 27.9 cm

26. *Feminine Fork* 2016
handmade paper over chicken wire, cast glitter on handmade paper, ground coal with matte medium
26 x 8 x 9 in 66 x 20.3 x 22.9 cm

27. *Lure* 2016
handmade paper over chicken wire, cast glitter on handmade paper, ground coal with matte medium
36 x 26 x 19 in 91.4 x 66 x 48.3 cm

28. *Double Scudder* 2016
handmade paper over chicken wire, cast glitter on handmade paper, ground coal with matte medium
25 x 29 x 16 in 63.5 x 73.7 x 40.6 cm

29. *Scudder Flip* 2016
handmade paper over chicken wire, ground coal with matte medium
36 x 24 x 17 1/2 in 91.4 x 61 x 44.5 cm

30. *Handmade Wax Off* 2014–16
handmade paper over chicken wire, ground coal with matte medium, acrylic, acrylic medium, glitter, gold leaf
27 x 10 x 9 in 68.6 x 25.4 x 22.9 cm

31. *Sparkle Devil* 2016
cast glitter on handmade paper over chicken wire
52 x 18 x 18 in 132.1 x 45.7 x 45.7 cm

32. *Storm a' Coming* 2016
handmade paper over chicken wire, cast glitter on handmade paper, ground coal with matte medium
27 x 32 x 15 in 68.6 x 81.3 x 38.1 cm

33. *Butterfly Jumper* 2016
handmade paper over chicken wire, cast glitter on handmade paper
40 x 30 x 16 in 101.6 x 76.2 x 40.6 cm

34. *Tres Group One* 2016
handmade paper over chicken wire
56 x 21 x 21 in 142.2 x 53.3 x 53.3 cm

35. *Old Soul One* 2016
cast glitter on handmade paper over chicken wire
38 x 25 x 20 in 96.5 x 63.5 x 50.8 cm

36. *Old Soul Two* 2016
handmade paper over chicken wire, cast glitter on handmade paper
32 x 34 x 17 in 81.3 x 86.4 x 43.2 cm

37. *Magic Growth* 2016
cast glitter on handmade paper over chicken wire
87 x 7 x 5 1/2 in 221 x 17.8 x 14 cm

38. *Dressed To Kill* 2016
handmade paper over chicken wire, cast glitter on handmade paper, ground coal with matte medium, acrylic medium, glitter
43 x 12 x 8 in 109.2 x 30.5 x 20.3 cm

39. *Uno (Shy Five)* 2016
cast glitter on handmade paper over chicken wire
55 x 15 x 14 in 139.7 x 38.1 x 35.6 cm

40. *Dos (Shy Five)* 2016
cast glitter on handmade paper over chicken wire
55 x 10 x 9 1/2 in 139.7 x 25.4 x 24.1 cm

41. *Tres (Shy Five)* 2016
cast glitter on handmade paper over chicken wire
54 x 11 x 15 in 137.2 x 27.9 x 38.1 cm

42. *Quatro (Shy Five)* 2016
cast glitter on handmade paper over chicken wire
54 x 16 x 13 in 137.2 x 40.6 x 33 cm

43. *Cinco (Shy Five)* 2016
cast glitter on handmade paper over chicken wire
47 x 15 x 17 1/2 in 119.4 x 38.1 x 44.5 cm

44. *Flacco Seis* 2016
cast glitter on handmade paper over chicken wire, ground coal with matte medium
56 x 13 x 9 in 142.2 x 33 x 22.9 cm

45. *First Double Sparkle Paper Totem* 2016
cast glitter on handmade paper over chicken wire, ground coal with matte medium
57 x 11 x 10 in 144.8 x 27.9 x 25.4 cm

46. *New Sparkle Jumper* 2016
handmade paper over chicken wire, cast glitter on handmade paper
32 x 25 x 18 in 81.3 x 63.5 x 45.7 cm

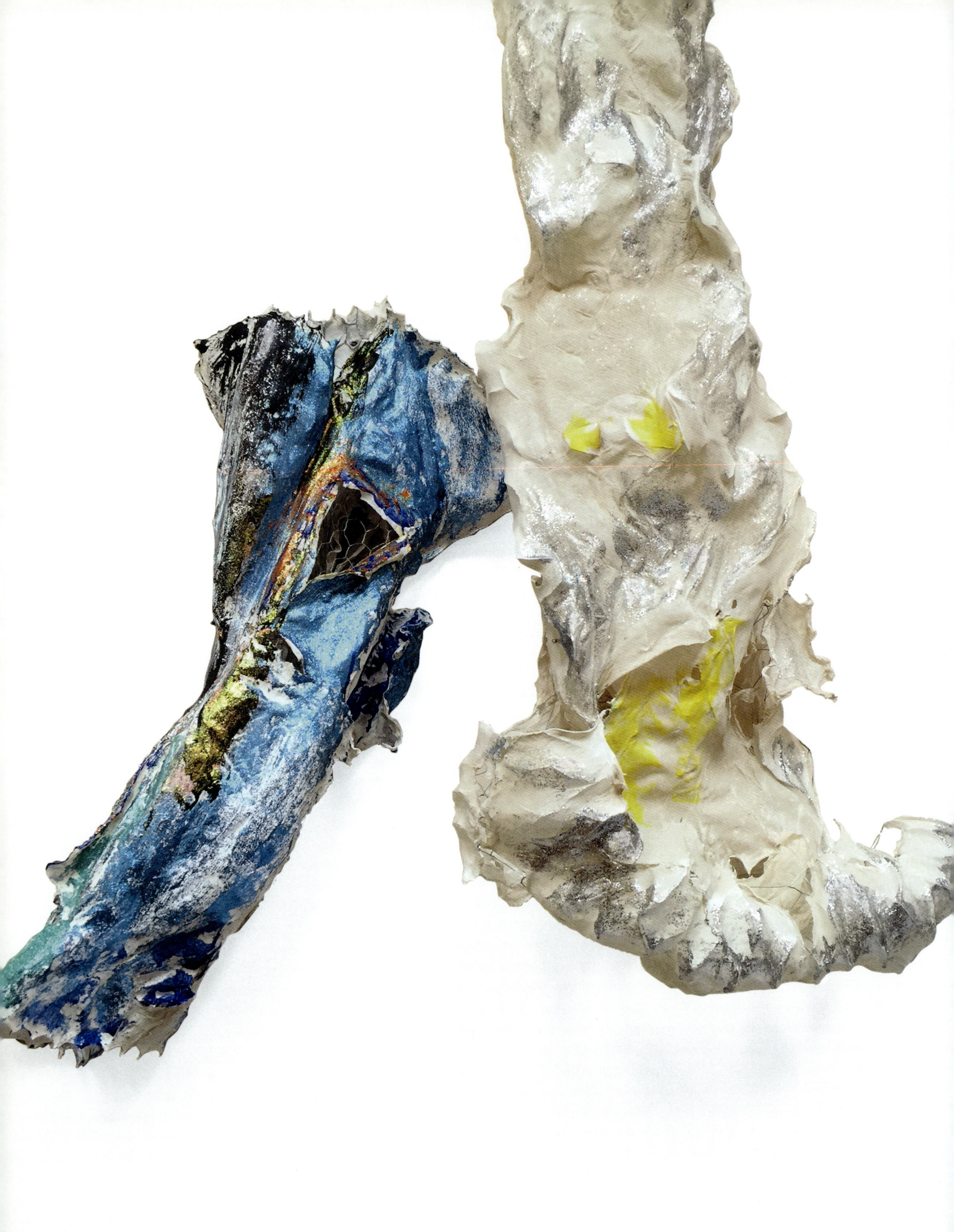

BIOGRAPHY

1941   Born in Lake Charles, Louisiana

1964   Newcomb College, B.F.A.

SOLO EXHIBITIONS

2016   *Lynda Benglis: New Work*, Cheim & Read, New York
Lynda Benglis, Bergen Assembly, Bergen, Norway
Cuerpos, Materia y Alma: Las Esculturas de Lynda Benglis, Museo International del Barroco, Puebla, Mexico
Lynda Benglis, Aspen Art Museum, Aspen, Colorado

2015   *Lynda Benglis*, The Hepworth Wakefield, Wakefield, United Kingdom
Lynda Benglis: Water Sources, Storm King Art Center, New Windsor, New York

2014   *Lynda Benglis*, Cheim & Read, New York
Lynda Benglis: Planar Device, Thomas Dane Gallery, London

2013   *Lynda Benglis: Everything Flows*, Locks Gallery, Philadelphia, Pennsylvania
Great Hall Exhibitions: Lynda Benglis, New York University Institute of Fine Arts, New York

2012   *Lynda Benglis*, Thomas Dane Gallery Gallery, London
Part One: New Works on Paper, Kappatos Gallery, Athens, Greece
Lynda Benglis: Figures, Savannah College of Art and Design Museum of Art, Savannah, Georgia
Lynda Benglis: Flow and Marks, Erich Hauser Art Foundation, Rottweil, Germany

2011   *Fountains*, Salon 94 Freemans, New York
Lynda Benglis: Glass Masks, Texas Gallery, Houston, Texas
Lynda Benglis, Museum of Contemporary Art, Los Angeles, California

2010   *Wax'in Wane*, Galerie Michael Janssen, Cologne, Germany
Flow and Flesh, Locks Gallery, Philadelphia, Pennsylvania

2009   *Lynda Benglis, New Work*, Cheim & Read, New York
Lynda Benglis, Van Abbemuseum, Eindhoven, Netherlands; traveled to the Irish

Museum of Modern Art, Dublin, Ireland; Museum le Consortium, Dijon, France; Museum of Art, Rhode Island School of Design, Providence, Rhode Island; New Museum, New York; The Museum of Contemporary Art, Los Angeles, California

2008   *Lynda Benglis: Shape Shifters*, Locks Gallery, Philadelphia, Pennsylvania
Lynda Benglis as Printmaker: A 30-Year Retrospective of Editions and Monotypes, Carl Solway Gallery, Cincinnati, Ohio

2007   *ArtMatters 11: Lynda Benglis*, McNay Art Museum, San Antonio, Texas
Lynda Benglis – Wax Paintings & Ceramic Sculptures, Texas Gallery, Houston, Texas

2006   *Lynda Benglis: Pleated, Knotted, Poured…*, Locks Gallery, Philadelphia, Pennsylvania
New Work by Lynda Benglis, Nina Freudenheim Gallery, Buffalo, New York

2005   *Lynda Benglis*, Susanne Hilberry Gallery, Ferndale, Michigan
Ceramic Sculpture, Frank Lloyd Gallery, Santa Monica, California

2004   *Lynda Benglis: A Sculpture Survey 1969–2004*, Cheim & Read, New York
Lynda Benglis: Ceramic Sculpture, Franklin Parrasch Gallery, New York

2003   *Lynda Benglis*, Toomey Tourell, San Francisco, California
Lynda Benglis: Sculptures, Bass Museum of Art, Miami, Florida

2002   *Lynda Benglis Soft Off*, Locks Gallery, Philadelphia, Pennsylvania
Small Bronzes and Wax Paintings, Cumberland Gallery, Nashville, Tennessee
Lynda Benglis: Ceramic Sculpture, Franklin Parrasch Gallery, New York

2001   *Echoes*, Riemba Gallery, Los Angeles, California
New Work, Toomey Tourell Gallery, San Francisco, California

2000   *Lynda Benglis*, Weatherspoon Gallery, University of North Carolina at Greensboro, North Carolina
Materials Girl, curated by Michael Klein, Meadows Museum, Shreveport, Louisiana
Lynda Benglis: A Decade of Ideas, Bryan Ohno Gallery, Seattle, Washington
Lynda Benglis: Hot Spots, Texas Gallery, Houston, Texas
Stacked, Forced, Pinched: Clay and Bronze Works by Lynda Benglis, Meadows Museum, Shreveport, Louisiana

1999   *Lynda Benglis, Small Works*, Galerie Simonne Stern, New Orleans, Louisiana
Lynda Benglis, Guild Hall Museum, East Hampton, New York
Lynda Benglis: New Work, Cheim & Read, New York

1998   *Lynda Benglis: Recent Sculpture and a Screening of "Female Sensibility" from 1973*,
Cheim & Read, New York
Lynda Benglis, Chimera, Forum Kunst Rottweil, Rottweil, Germany; traveled to
Galerie Six Friedrich, Munich, Germany; Charim Klocker Gallery, Vienna, Austria
Dynamic Silhouette, Kappatos Gallery, Athens, Greece
Lynda Benglis: Selected Wall Reliefs, USF Contemporary Art Museum, University of
South Florida, Tampa, Florida

1997   *Selected Wall Reliefs*, Elizabeth Mayer Fine Art, New York
Hidden Agenda, Contemporary Art Gallery, Ahmedabad, India
Lynda Benglis, Galerie Michael Janssen, Cologne, Germany
Lynda Benglis Glass, Dorfman Projects, New York

1996   *Lynda Benglis: Ceramics*, Porter Troupe Gallery, San Diego, California
New Monotypes: Landscapes & Fetishes, Quartet Editions, New York

1995   *Lynda Benglis: Recent Wall & Glass Sculpture*, Heath Gallery, Atlanta, Georgia
Lynda Benglis, Galerie Simonne Stern, New Orleans, Louisiana
Lynda Benglis: Sculpture, Susanne Hilberry Gallery, Birmingham, Michigan

1994   *Wax Paintings*, Paula Cooper Gallery, New York
Lynda Benglis: Wax Paintings, Heath Gallery, Atlanta
Chimera: Recent Ceramic Sculpture, The Harwood Foundation Museum, Taos,
New Mexico; traveled to Boulder Museum of Art, Boulder, Colorado;
Cranbrook Art Museum, Bloomfield Hills, Michigan; University Gallery, New
Mexico State University, Las Cruces, New Mexico

1993   *Clothed and Unclothed: Recent Sculpture*, Richard Gray Gallery, Chicago, Illinois
From the Furnace, Auckland City Art Center, Auckland, New Zealand
Ceramic Sculpture, Tavelli Gallery, Aspen, Colorado
Lynda Benglis, Gow Langsford Gallery, Auckland, New Zealand

1992   *Lynda Benglis: Recent Work*, Heath Gallery, Atlanta, Georgia

1991   *Recent Work*, Heath Gallery, Atlanta, Georgia
Lynda Benglis: Dual Natures, Retrospective, The High Museum of Art, Atlanta,
Georgia; traveled to Contemporary Arts Center & New Orleans Museum of
Art, New Orleans, Louisiana; San Jose Museum of Art, San Jose, California
New Works, Tilden Foley Gallery, New Orleans, Louisiana
Lynda Benglis, Margo Leavin Gallery, Los Angeles, California

1990   *Lynda Benglis: Recent Sculpture*, Richard Gray Gallery, Chicago, Illinois

Lynda Benglis: *Sculpture and Silk Paintings*, Linda Farris Gallery, Seattle, Washington
Lynda Benglis, Sena Galleries West, Santa Fe, New Mexico
Lynda Benglis: *Tropies*, Paula Cooper Gallery, New York

1989   *Drawing with Materials: Process and Image. Works by Lynda Benglis*, Hester Merwin
Ayers Gallery, Atlantic Center for the Arts, Smyrna Beach, Florida
Lynda Benglis, Tilden-Foley Gallery, New Orleans, Louisiana
Lynda Benglis: New Sculpture, Margo Leavin Gallery, Los Angeles, California
Florida Fan Dance: A Palmetto Series. Monotype Prints by Lynda Benglis, Michael
Murphy Gallery, Tampa, Florida

1988   *Lynda Benglis: Recent Sculpture and Works on Paper*, Cumberland Gallery, Nashville,
Tennessee
Lynda Benglis, Full Gross Gallery, San Francisco, California

1987   *Lynda Benglis: Recent Sculpture*, Paula Cooper Gallery, New York
Lynda Benglis: Monoprints/Windy Hill Series, Landfall Press, New York
Lynda Benglis: New Sculpture, Margo Leavin Gallery, Los Angeles, California

1986   *Lynda Benglis*, Fuller Goldeen Gallery, San Francisco, California
Lynda Benglis, Tilden-Foley Gallery, New Orleans, Louisiana
Lynda Benglis: Glass, Dart Gallery, Chicago, Illinois

1985   *Lynda Benglis: Works in Glass*, Margo Leavin Gallery, Los Angeles, California
Lynda Benglis: New Works in Glass, Susanne Hilberry Gallery, Birmingham, Michigan
Glass, Dart Gallery, Chicago, Illinois
Lynda Benglis: Recent Wall Pieces and Glass Sculpture, Heath Gallery, Atlanta, Georgia

1984   *Lynda Benglis: New Sculpture*, Paula Cooper Gallery, New York
Lynda Benglis: New Sculptures, Texas Gallery, Houston, Texas
Lynda Benglis: New Sculpture, Tilden-Foley Gallery, New Orleans, Louisiana

1983   *Lynda Benglis: New Sculpture*, Susanne Hilberry Gallery, Birmingham, Michigan
Lynda Benglis, Dart Gallery, Chicago, Illinois

1982   *Lynda Benglis*: *Sculpture and Works on Paper*, Okun-Thomas Gallery, St. Louis, Missouri
Lynda Benglis: Flux & Fusion, Margo Leavin Gallery, Los Angeles, California
Benglis: ΕΙΩΛΑ, Paula Cooper Gallery, New York
Lynda Benglis, Fuller Goldeen Gallery, San Francisco, California

1981   *Lynda Benglis*: *Drawings from India*, Museum of Art, University of Arizona, Tucson, Arizona
Lynda Benglis: *Indian Wood Blocks*, Galerie Albert Baronian, Brussels, Beligum

Lynda Benglis: New Work, Dart Gallery, Chicago, Illinois
Lynda Benglis: *Recent Gold Pieces*, Jacksonville Art Museum, Florida
Lynda Benglis: Sculptures, Texas Gallery, Houston, Texas
Lynda Benglis, Cirrus Gallery, Los Angeles, California

1980   *Lynda Benglis 1968–1978*, University of South Florida, Tampa, Florida;
traveled to the Lowe Art Museum, University of Miami, Coral Gables, Florida
Lynda Benglis, Margo Leavin Gallery, Los Angeles, California
Recent Works by Lynda Benglis, Portland Center for the Visual Arts, Portland, Oregon
*Fans (Air) Kites (Air) Airport (Air). Lynda Benglis: "Patang." The Atlanta Airport
Commission and New Works Executed in Ahmedabad*, India, Texas Gallery, Houston, Texas
Lynda Benglis: Aquanots, Paula Cooper Gallery, New York
Lynda Benglis: Recent Works, Heath Gallery, Atlanta
Lynda Benglis, Woodland Gallery, Chatham College, Pittsburgh, Pennsylvania
Lynda Benglis: New Work, Susanne Hilberry Gallery, Birmingham, Michigan

1979   *Lynda Benglis: New Works*, Texas Gallery, Houston, Texas
Lynda Benglis: New Works, Dart Gallery, Chicago, Illinois
Lynda Benglis: *Wall Sculptures and Floor Installations*, Real Art Ways, New
Haven, Connecticut
Lynda Benglis: Bodies and Fans, Hansen-Fuller Goldeen Gallery, San Francisco, California
Lynda Benglis: *Recent Works*, Georgia State University, Atlanta, Georgia
Lynda Benglis, Galerie Albert Baronian, Brussels, Belgium
Lynda Benglis, Paula Cooper Gallery, New York

1978   *Lynda Benglis*, Paula Cooper Gallery, New York

1977   *Lynda Benglis Presents Amazing Bow-Wow*, The Kitchen, New York
The Amazing Bow Wow, Thomas Lewallen Gallery, Venice, California
7 Come 11: A Series of Recent Sculpture by Lynda Benglis, Margo Leavin Gallery,
Los Angeles, California
Lynda Benglis: *Copper Knots and Floor Sculpture*, Douglas Drake Gallery, Kansas
City, Missouri

1976   *Lynda Benglis: Metallized Knots and Wax Paintings*, Paula Cooper Gallery, Los
Angeles, California
Videotapes, AND/OR, Seattle, Washington

1975   *Physical and Psychological Moments in Time: A First Retrospective of the Video
Work of Lynda Benglis*, Fine Arts Center Gallery, State University of New York
College at Oneonta, New York
Video Polaroids, The Kitchen, New York

Lynda Benglis: Sculpture, Paula Cooper Gallery, New York
Lynda Benglis, Texas Gallery, Houston, Texas

1974   *Lynda Benglis Presents Metallized Knots*, Paula Cooper Gallery, New York
Lynda Benglis: Knots, Hansen-Fuller Gallery, San Francisco, California

1973   *Video Tapes*, Paula Cooper Gallery, New York
Lynda Benglis Video Tapes, Video Gallery, Everson Museum of Art, Syracuse, New York
Lynda Benglis: Paintings and Videotapes, Hansen-Fuller Gallery, San Francisco, California
Dimensional Paintings by Lynda Benglis, Portland Center for the Visual Arts, Oregon
Lynda Benglis, Texas Gallery, Houston, Texas
Lynda Benglis, Jack Glenn Gallery, Corona Del Mar, California
Lynda Benglis, The Clocktower, the Institute for Art and Urban Resources, New York

1972   *Wax Paintings*, Hansen-Fuller Gallery, San Francisco

1971   *The Kansas State University Union Art Gallery and the Kansas State University
Department of Art Invitational Exhibition '71*, Union Art Galleries, Kansas State
University, Manhattan, Kansas
Lynda Benglis, Paula Cooper Gallery, New York
Lynda Benglis: Polyurethane Foam, Two-Component System, Hayden Gallery,
Massachusetts Institute of Technology, Cambridge, Massachusetts

1970   *Lynda Benglis*, Paula Cooper Gallery, New York
Lynda Benglis, Janie C. Lee Gallery, Dallas, Texas
Lynda Benglis, Galerie Hans Müller, Cologne, Germany

1969   *Lynda Benglis*, University of Rhode Island, Kingston, Rhode Island

2015   *Free Fall: Lynda Benglis and Polly Apfelbaum*, Locks Gallery, Philadelphia, Pennsylvania

2012   *Lynda Benglis and Georgia O'Keefe: A Dialogue Across Time*, Georgia O' Keefe Museum, Santa Fe, New Mexico

2009   *Lynda Benglis/Robert Morris: 1973–1974*, Susan Inglett Gallery, New York

2007   *Circa 70: Lynda Benglis and Louise Bourgeois*, Cheim & Read, New York

2005   *Monique Prieto: New Paintings & Lynda Benglis: The Graces*, Cheim & Read, New York

2004   *Improvisation: Lynda Benglis and Isaac Witkin*, Locks Gallery, Philadelphia, Pennsylvania

2002   *Bettina Rheims/Lynda Benglis*, Cheim & Read, New York
Small Bronze and Wax Paintings by Lynda Benglis and Images from Mexico, Photographs by Jack Spencer, Cumberland Gallery, Nashville, Tennessee

1999   *Lynda Benglis – Wols: Photographs of the 1930s*, Cheim & Read, New York
Lynda Benglis – Joe Zucker, Guild Hall Museum, East Hampton, New York

1989   *American Sculptures, NY & LA (with Mark Lere)*, Kamakura Gallery, Tokyo, Japan

1988   *Lynda Benglis – Ida Kohlmeyer*, Cumberland Gallery, Nashville, Tennessee

1987   *Ida Kohlmeyer/Lynda Benglis: Teacher and Student in the 80's*, Gibson Barkam Gallery, Imperial Calcasieu Museum, Lake Charles, Louisiana; traveled to Pensacola Museum of Art, Florida
Lynda Benglis & Keith Sonnier: A Ten Year Retrospective, 1977–1987, Alexandria Museum of Art, Alexandria, Louisiana

1985   *Kohlmeyer and Benglis: Teacher and Student in the '80s*, Pensacola Museum of Art, Pensacola, Florida

1983   *Recent Work: Lynda Benglis & John Duff*, Margo Leavin Gallery, Los Angeles, California

1979   Susanne Hilberry Gallery, Birmingham, Michigan (with Ron Gorchov)

1977   Hansen-Fuller Gallery, San Francisco, California (with William Weege)

1971   *Lynda Benglis: Plastiken. Allan Hacklin: Bilder*, Forum Kunst Rottweil, Rottweil, Germany

1970   Virginia Polytechnic Institute, Blacksburg, Virginia (with Michael Goldberg)

Cerrillos, New Mexico studio, 2016.

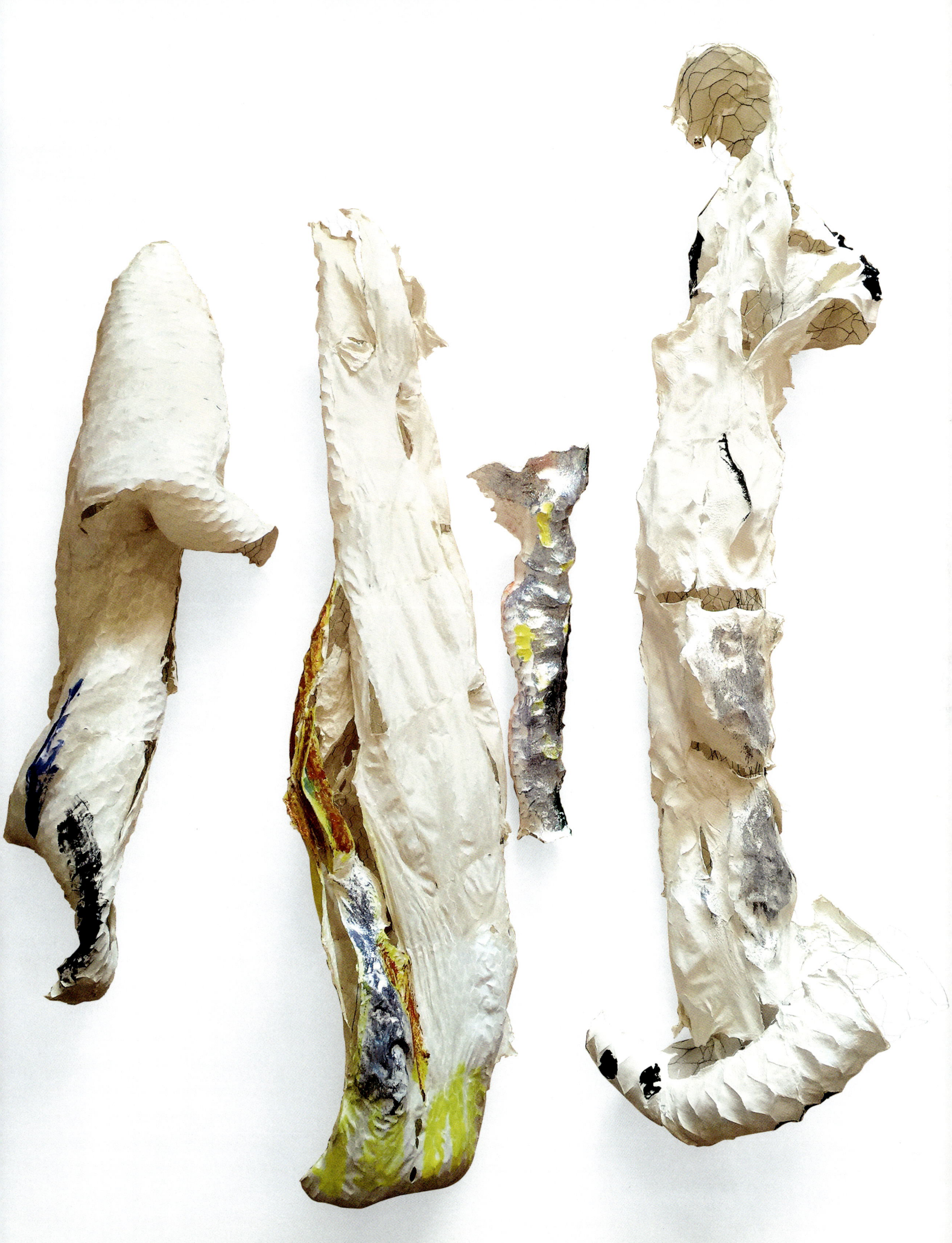

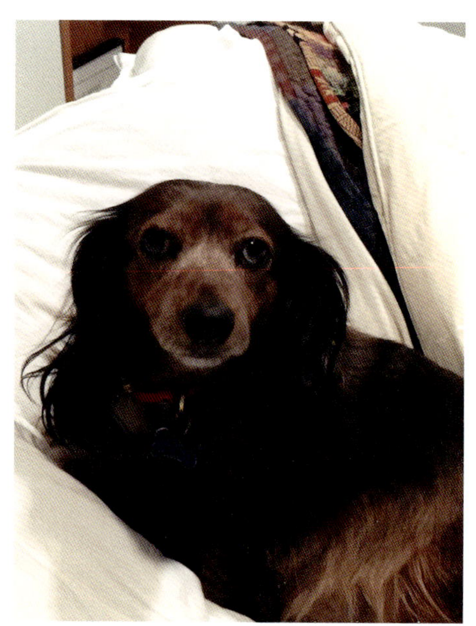

Dedicated to Pi.

Front cover: Feminine Fork, 2016, handmade paper over chicken wire, cast glitter on handmade paper, ground coal with matte medium, 26 x 8 x 9 in 66 x 20.3 x 22.9 cm, (detail). Back cover: Torn Totem, 2015, handmade paper over chicken wire, 90 x 13 x 20 in 228.6 x 33 x 50.8 cm, (detail). Frontispiece: Old Sparkle Tongue, 2015-16, handmade paper over chicken wire, acrylic, glitter, 29 x 5 1/2 x 6 in 73.7 x 14 x 15.2 cm (detail). Opposite title page: Gone Harlequin, 2016, handmade paper over chicken wire, cast glitter on handmade paper, ground coal with matte medium, 87 x 9 x 8 in 221 x 22.9 x 20.3 cm (detail). Louise Bourgeois, Fillette, 1968. Photo: Allan Finkelman, © The Easton Foundation/Licensed by VAGA, NY. Jackson Pollock, Phosphorescence, 1947, Collection Addison Gallery of American Art, Gift of Peggy Guggenheim. © 2016 The Pollock-Krasner Foundation/Artists Rights Society (ARS), NY. Louisiana Prop Piece, 1977, courtesy the New Orleans Museum of Art. Art © Lynda Benglis/Licensed by VAGA, New York.

Photography: Brian Buckley

Photography Post-Production: Morgan Palmer

ISBN 978–1–944316–04–4

Printed in Italy by Trifolio

Printed in an edition of 2,000
on the occasion of the 2016 exhibition

Lynda Benglis

Cheim & Read

Text Nancy Princenthal

Design John Cheim

Editor Ellen Robinson